Chocolate Cosmos,
String of Pearls

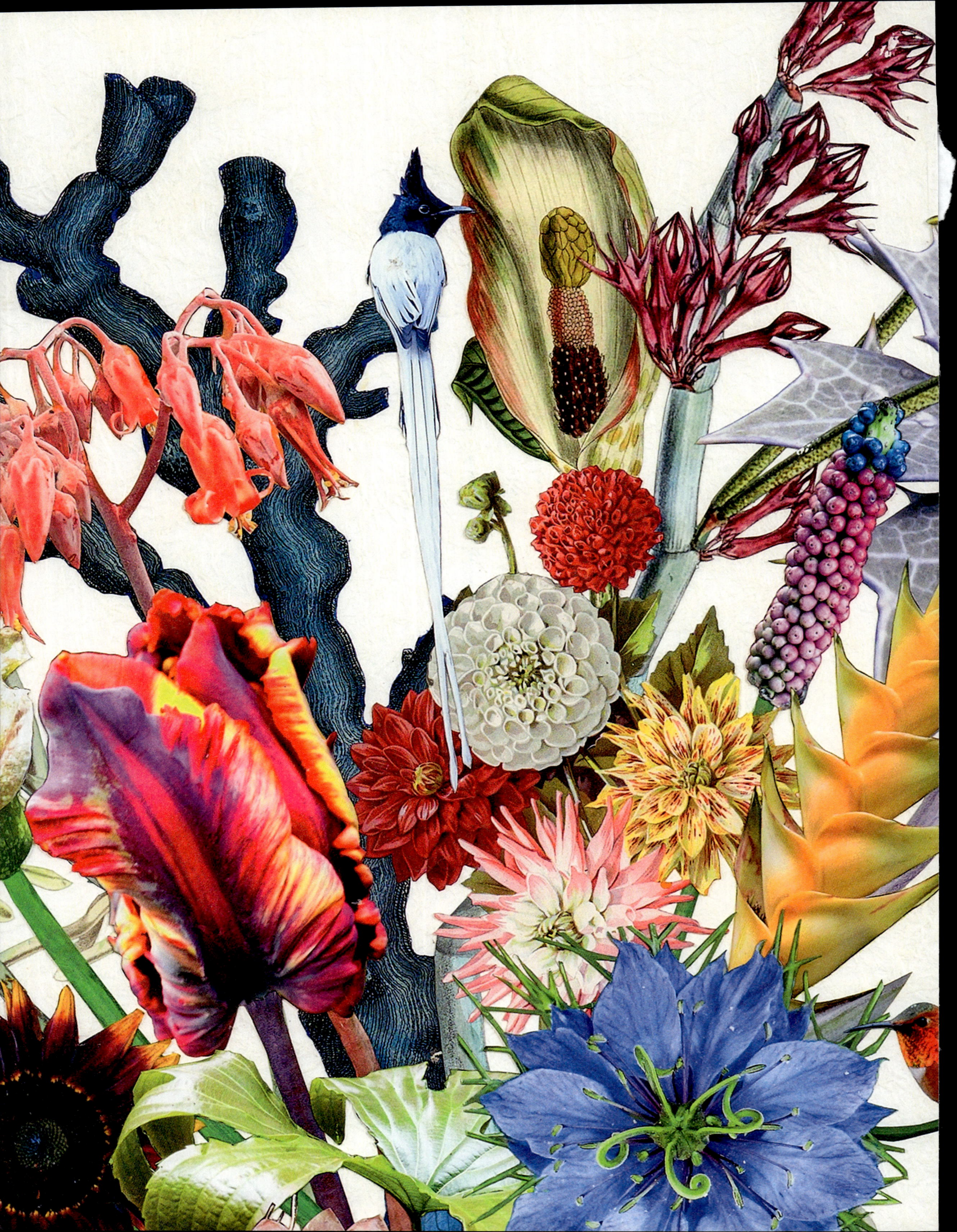

Jane Hammond

Chocolate Cosmos, String of Pearls

HURTWOOD

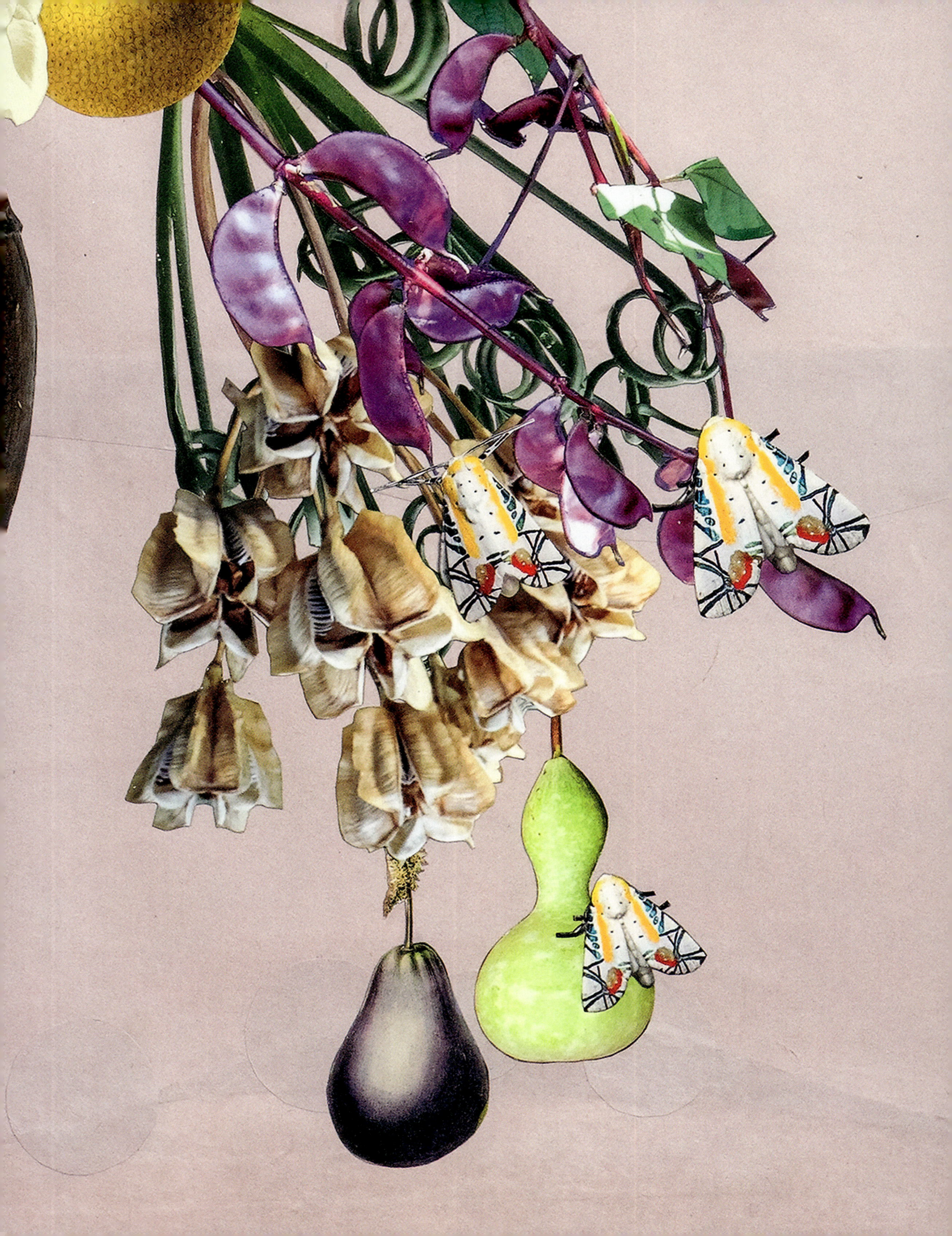

Contents

Previous page:
***San Francisco Yacht Club Trophy with Paradise Flycatcher, Nigella and Xerces Blues*, 2023 (detail)**
Unique botanical collage using digital printing, coloured pencil, Sumi ink, watercolour and gouache, hand cut and assembled on collaged Japanese papers over painted cotton rag
106.7 × 88.9 cm
42 × 35 in

***Martaban Jar with Prairie Smoke, Witch Hazel and Three Picasso Moths*, 2025 (detail)**
Unique botanical collage using relief printing, linocut, digital printing, coloured pencil, Sumi ink, watercolour and gouache, hand cut and assembled on collaged Japanese papers over cotton rag
127 × 96.5 cm
50 × 38 in

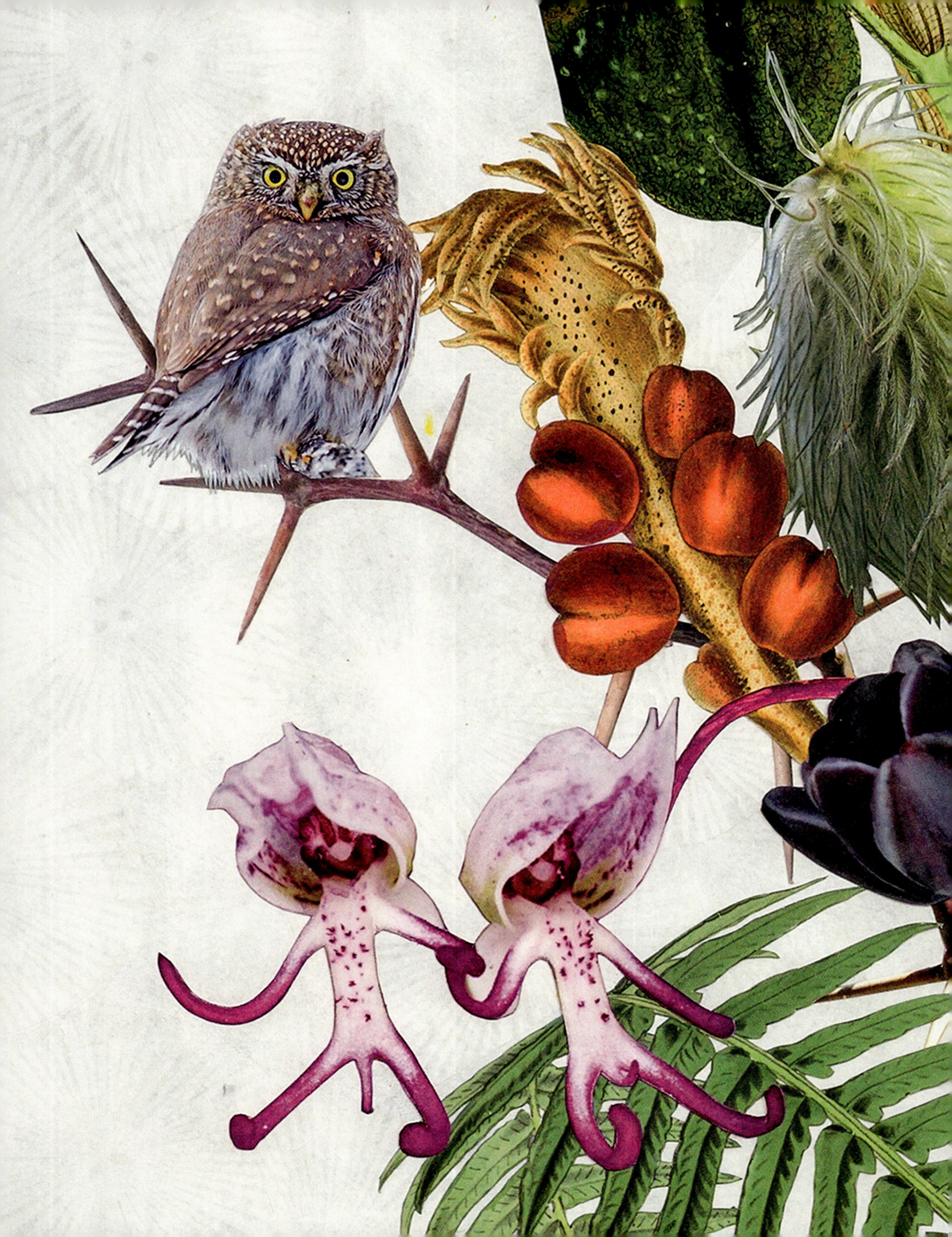

Foreword
John Berggruen

Jane Hammond continues to amaze me with the constant evolution of her work. She possesses an innate talent for painting and collage, as well as a strong sense of individuality in her artistic practice. During my most recent visit to Jane's studio, I was guided through the meticulously organised piles of cut-outs, drawings and prints that form essential components of her alluring botanical compositions.

We've been lucky enough to have had three solo exhibitions with Jane, and working together over the years has been both a pleasure and a fantastic partnership that has fostered many loyal collectors. She is a rare talent, and the work in this show and this book – *Chocolate Cosmos, String of Pearls* – demonstrates her capacity to create art that is uplifting, beautiful and profoundly complex.

Significantly, Jane's work is held in the permanent collections of over eighty institutions across the USA, among them the Art Institute of Chicago, the Fine Arts Museums of San Francisco, the Museum of Fine Arts, Houston, the Museum of Modern Art, New York City, and the Whitney Museum of American Art.

Collaborating on this book has been a wonderful opportunity to showcase her artistic vision and marks an important milestone in her career. I would like to thank Jane for her energy and brilliance, as well as the acclaimed writer Jenny Uglow for her extended essay presented here. I would also like to thank Francis Atterbury and his team at Hurtwood Press for making this beautiful book possible.

***Roman Glass with Prairie Anemone, Naked Man Orchid and Pygmy Owl*, 2022 (detail)**
Unique botanical collage using relief printing, digital printing, coloured pencil, Sumi ink, watercolour and gouache, hand cut and assembled on collaged Japanese papers over painted cotton rag
127 × 96.5 cm
50 × 38 in

Venetian Glass with Hellebore, Hearts-a-bustin' and Black Tulip
2022 (detail)
Unique botanical collage using linocut, digital printing, coloured pencil, Sumi ink, watercolour and gouache, hand cut and assembled on collaged Japanese papers over cotton rag
71.1 × 98.4 cm
28 × 38¾ in

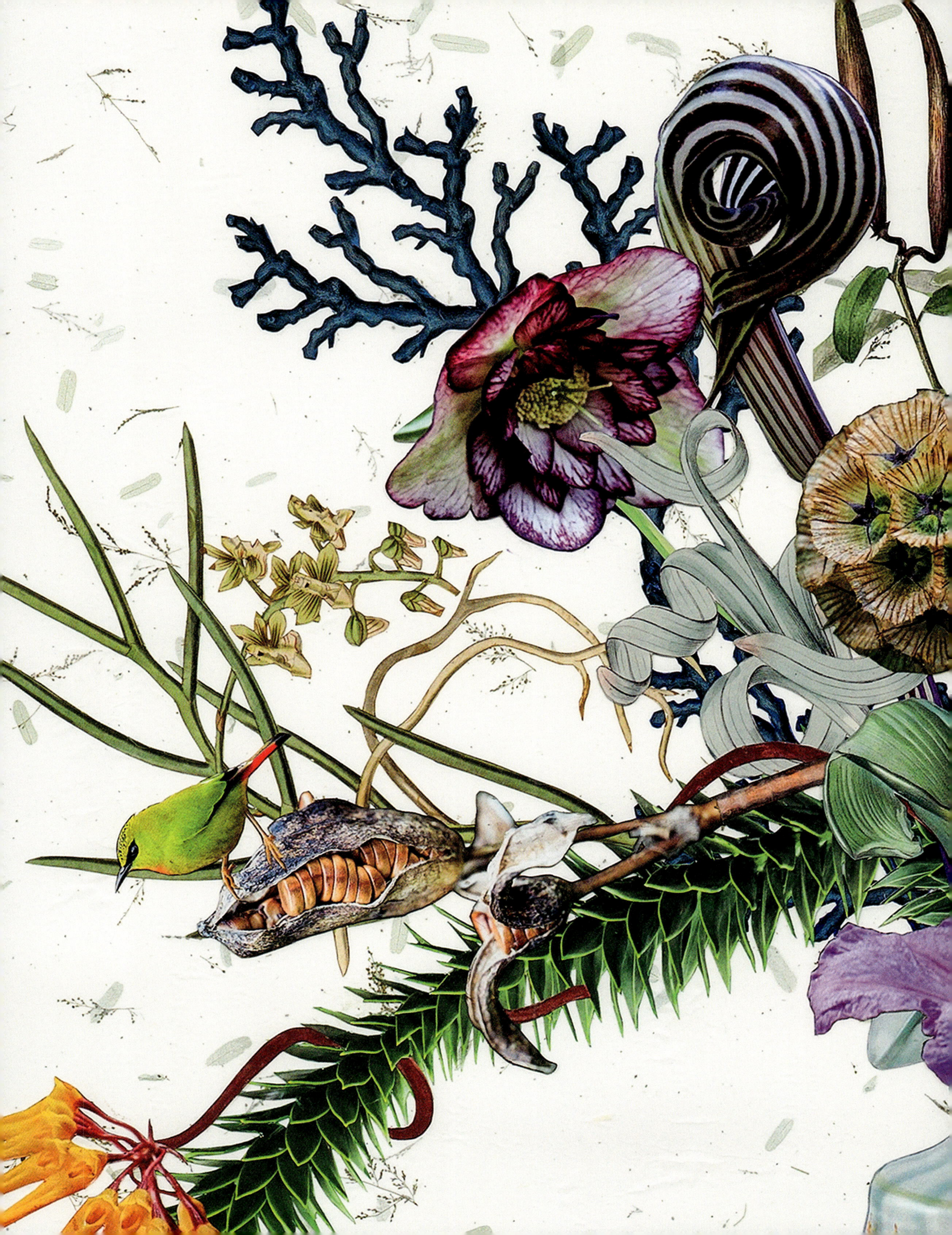

New Botanical Works
Jenny Uglow

Jane Hammond's botanical collages are rhythmic, vibrant, strangely alive. They are utterly original, yet their spectacular arrangements of images of flowers, grasses, seeds, accompanied by insects and birds, are also curiously familiar, offering a fresh take on a great tradition.

All Hammond's work is a dialogue with the culture we inherit and inhabit, a reshaping of the images that surround us. A supreme paper-artist, whose work can be found in major galleries and museums in the USA and abroad, Hammond is a painter, printmaker, photographer and sculptor, as well as a collagist. In a short video for the Metropolitan Museum in New York, talking of her fascination with the way old photographs catch unscripted dramas, she describes herself as 'having a diverse practice collecting found information and transforming it'. This transformation takes many forms: sometimes she plays with narrative; elsewhere she lets discrete, unnamed images form random associations – their 'meaning' is in the eye of the beholder. Her *Butterfly Maps*, such as *All Souls (Canterbury)* and the gilded scraps in *Loose Tapestry of Daily Life (Rotary Phone)*, from 2014, convey both the fragility and continuity of human history. She has long been interested, too, in the diverse ways that images preserve and present information, and in the convention and context of display, as in the *Scrapbook* series of 2003–06, or *Tabula Rosa* (2001), where the ground was her own body.

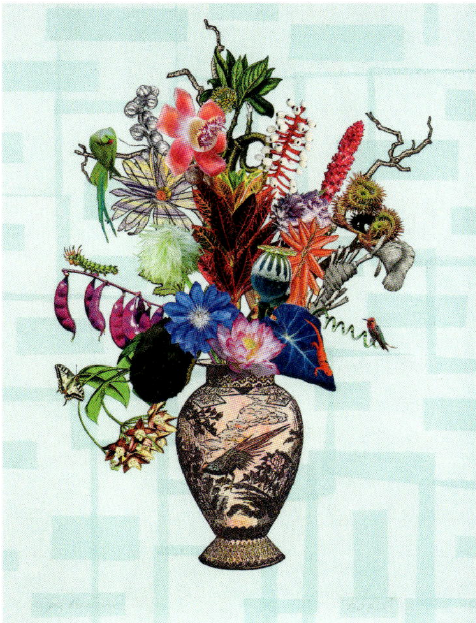

***Chinese Bird Vase with Cannonball Tree Flower, Red Eft and Doll's Eyes*, 2022**
Unique botanical collage using relief printing, digital printing, coloured pencil, Sumi ink, watercolour, gouache and mica, hand cut and assembled on collaged Japanese papers over cotton rag
127 × 96.5 cm
50 × 38 in

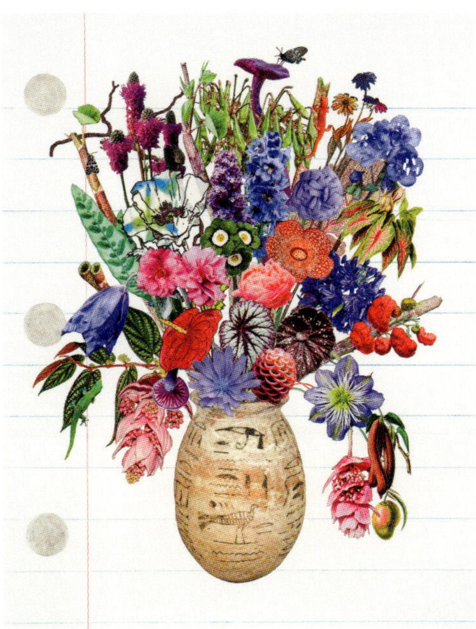

***Egyptian Vase with Sow Thistle, Amethyst Deceiver and Himalayan Balsam*, 2025**
Unique botanical collage using relief printing, linocut, digital printing, coloured pencil, Sumi ink, watercolour and gouache, hand cut and assembled on collaged Japanese papers over painted cotton rag
127 × 96.5 cm
50 × 38 in

The convention that she explores in her floral collages looks back to the first great age of Dutch flower painting. In Ambrosius Bosschaert the Elder's *Still Life of Flowers in a Wan-Li Vase on a Ledge with Further Flowers, Shells and a Butterfly* (1609–10), the fixed, monochrome form of the bird on the vase (like those on Hammond's *Chinese Bird Vase with Cannonball Tree Flower, Red Eft and Doll's Eyes*, 2022, or *Egyptian Vase with Sow Thistle, Amethyst Deceiver and Himalayan Balsam*, 2025) contrasts with the radiant illusionism of the painting. The genre allowed artists to show their skill in mimicking textures and surfaces, light and sheen, yet the tangled stems, buds and blooms were never a reflection of reality. The Dutch paintings, intended to entertain botanists and rich collectors, depicted specimens from different countries and continents, plants that would never bloom in the same place and at the same time. Similarly, Hammond brings together images and techniques from myriad places and times: old calendars, cards and prints, wrapping paper and cloth, lithography, linocuts, relief printing, digital printing, watercolour, gouache and more. This is a 'found', unnatural realm.

Flower painting quickly became associated with women artists, like Rachel Ruysch, whose romantic, asymmetrical compositions, with jewel-like insects and glowing flowers against sombre backgrounds, burned with energy while implying the transience of this glory, the theme of '*Vanitas*'. Women also depicted flowers in embroidery and domestic crafts; the great cut-paper artist Mary Delany was a skilled embroiderer before she told her niece, at the age of seventy-three in 1772: 'I have invented a new way of imitating flowers.' She went on to make nearly a thousand 'paper mosaicks', astounding for their botanical accuracy, calling them her *Herbal* or *Hortus Siccus*, a collection of dried flowers. Some were made from hundreds of tiny pieces, carefully layered and glued, becoming increasingly lifelike, as in the *Rosa Gallica* with an insect bite on its leaf. Delany collected and treasured different kinds of paper – as Hammond does today – and her skill in cutting was supreme, another feature that Hammond shares: 'I have more pairs of scissors than anyone I know,' she laughs.

Botany itself was considered a woman's subject. Self-taught women naturalists collected butterflies, ferns, grasses, seaweed and shells and arranged their pressed plant specimens in albums and commonplace books. The delight was both scientific and sensual: Victorian women painted their finds in watercolours, made decorative arrangements in folded and cut paper, and created boxes and books. At the same time, natural images invaded textiles, wallpaper and printed china: the dresses women wore, the plates they ate off, the rooms they lived in, all abounded in flowers. In the twentieth century, flower arranging itself became a recognised art.

The long, feminine legacy touches Hammond's own life: these collages spring, she thinks, partly from her childhood, much of which she spent with her grandmother, an innocent and hugely ambitious gardener, who made her learn the Latin names of a hundred plants when she was six – she can still remember some now. She has always been interested in taxonomy and natural forms. Her very titles have an evocative, taxonomic twang, while echoing the solemn precision of their early Dutch forebears, like Jan van Huysum's *Glass Vase with Flowers, with a Poppy and a Finch Nest* (c. 1720–21). They roll in the mouth with poetic resonance:

> *Mosque Lamp with Nightingale, Cardoons and Leopard Frog*
> *Persian Cameo Glass with Blue Macaw, Monster Beans and Monkey Puzzle Tree*
> *Choctaw Carrying Basket with Bat Lily, Axinaea and Green Cone-Headed Plant Hopper*
> *Han Dynasty Cocoon Jar with Chocolate Cosmos, Roseate Parakeet and Blushing Philodendron.*

Unlike her grandmother, Hammond has no garden. Instead, huge welded cantilevered ledges, full of plants, hang from the windows of her Manhattan flat. Defying a cold spring, for instance, hellebores and cyclamen flower among millet and boxwood. Her inner, artist's garden is full too, of representations of plants: drawers, cupboards and boxes overflow with a huge stockpile of images, gathered over the years, ready for her to harvest at will.

Part of the intensity and appeal of the botanical collages comes from the contrasting styles and divergent origins of the images: a tiny daisy from a wrapping paper design, an angular twig from a plantsman's catalogue, a flycatcher from an old print, a pale camellia from a floral handkerchief. Each found image has its own 'embedded sense of time', often at odds with other elements. In a talk at Berggruen Gallery in 2025 Hammond explained how the disparate materials impart a tension to the work: 'What I'm interested in is wrenching a harmony, a kind of ensemble, made of tension, and difference, and friction – you get this oscillation in your mind between unity and disunity – it's more like life itself.' The mobile, shimmering balance is important to her, she says, 'and that's what collage does best'. Unlikely bedfellows meet in surprising sympathy, discords and clashes make a piece hum, and the intricate, bizarre natural forms attain an abstract quality. The three-dimensional effect also makes the collages almost hyperreal, involving the viewer in a special way. The eye ricochets around, from detail to detail, and there is a constant see-saw between tension and harmony as the varied media produce different effects, reflections and textures.

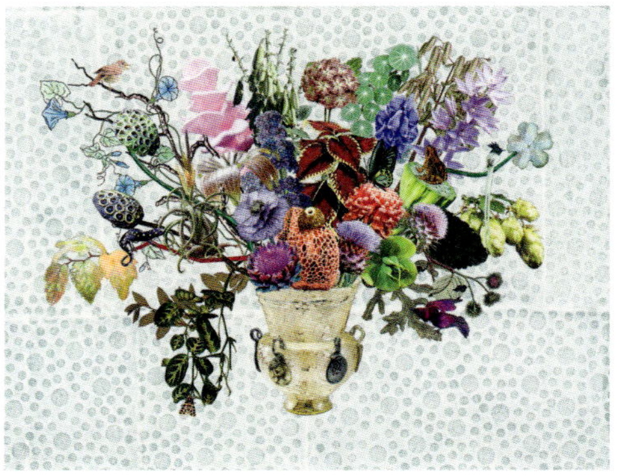

Mosque Lamp with Nightingale, Cardoons and Leopard Frog, 2024
Unique botanical collage with relief print, digital printing, coloured pencil, Sumi ink, watercolour and gouache, hand cut and assembled on collaged Thai papers over painted cotton rag
96.5 × 127 cm
38 × 50 in

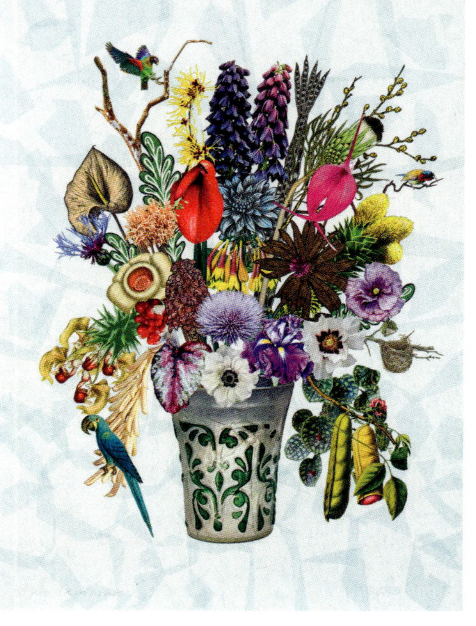

Persian Cameo Glass with Blue Macaw, Monster Beans and Monkey Puzzle Tree, 2025
Unique botanical collage using relief printing, linocut, digital printing, coloured pencil, Sumi ink, watercolour and gouache, hand cut and assembled on collaged Japanese papers over cotton rag
127 × 96.5 cm
50 × 38 in

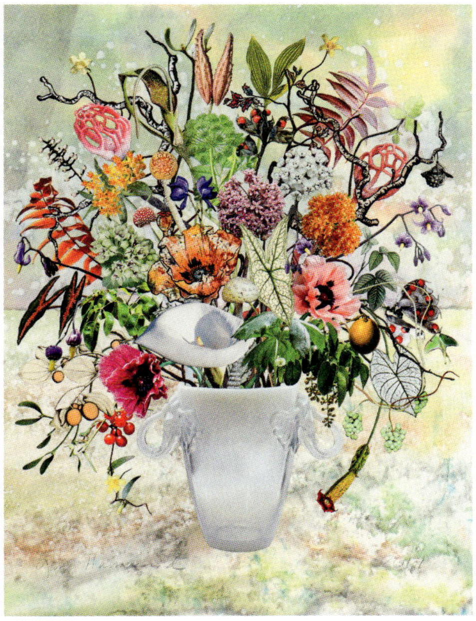

***Elephant Vase with Basket Stinkhorn, Heartbreak Grass and Strychnine*, 2017**
Unique botanical collage using lithography, linocut, relief printing, digital printing, coloured pencil, Sumi ink, watercolour and gouache, hand cut and assembled on collaged hand-painted Japanese papers over cotton rag
127 × 96.5 cm
50 × 38 in

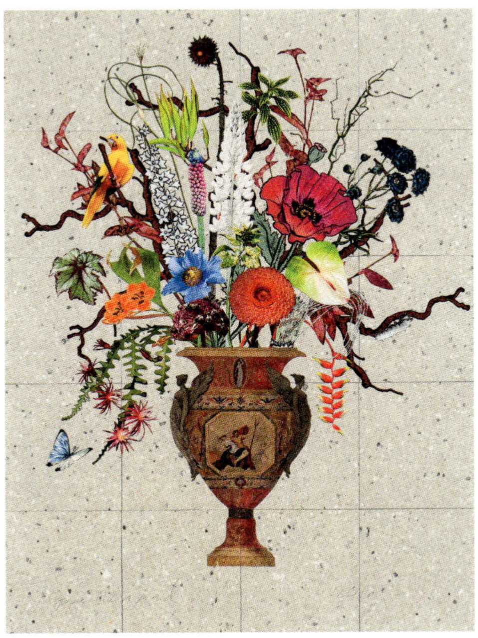

***Spanish Vase with Thistle, Angelica and Lupine*, 2016**
Unique botanical collage using lithography, linocut, relief printing, digital printing, coloured pencil, Sumi ink, watercolour, gouache and gold leaf, hand cut and assembled on Japanese papers over painted cotton rag
127 × 96.5 cm
50 × 38 in

Hammond's collages look carefree and spontaneous, but they demand phenomenal care and application. The arrangement is everything. With collage you are not committed as you would be to a drawing, where a line on paper is final. Here you can pick and choose, select and discard, place and move. As she says, 'It's a really vexatious problem for quite a long time – then suddenly, it's a winner. Or you can feel it is ninety percent done, but the final detail won't come, and then you are utterly flummoxed and have to take the whole thing apart and start again.' To glue, or not to glue? – that is the question. But then, miraculously, it feels right. Then comes a final stage, touching up with watercolour to bring out the green on a twig, the deeper blue of a flower's centre.

Although Hammond's sense of design feels intuitive, her work is in essence conceptual and intellectual. All the collages come from what she calls 'a germ' (a typically organic term). Sometimes this can be expressed verbally, as with *Elephant Vase with Basket Stinkhorn, Heartbreak Grass and Strychnine* (2017), where the key word is 'poison'. In this colourful arrangement everything can bring harm, not only the deadly nightshade and the little green leaves of the Florida Poisonwood tree, but the opium poppies, the stinking voodoo lily, the veined white leaves of Caladium that swell the throat, the mistletoe and mandrake. Dame Nature, the piece jests, can be a genuine *femme fatale.*

While some 'germs' are nameable, others are aesthetic. Hammond found the idea for *Korean Vase with Hyacinth Beans, Cotton and Chrysanthemum* (2016) when she saw a hellebore with a bruise-like shadow. Inspired, she set to work with a 'bruised palette', its discomfort conveyed by the prickly cotton heads offset by highlights of various greens and purples, including the rich magenta hyacinth beans. For the extraordinary background, Hammond painted the mother-sheet grey and used Japanese papers with a script, working vertically – another tantalising element, another implied story. The Korean vase, too, is a dulled silver with bronze, not the 'ingratiating shiny silver' one might expect.

The vases play an important part, harking back, perhaps, to Hammond's graduate work in ceramics. The intriguing urn in *Spanish Vase with Thistle, Angelica and Lupin* (2016), was found by her husband, a digital image of a gouache painting from a library in Madrid. A slight line, showing where the page was folded, made Hammond think of tiles, which she then used for the background: their hard surface shows off the colours and texture of the plant images, while their square shape also makes the bifurcation of the vase an element of the whole design. There are many sets of reflections here: a tall thistle and strangely right-angled twig hint at the trident carried by the man in the vase painting, the red flowers echo his scarlet cloak, the white lupin reflects the woman's dress. Similarly, the vase's symmetrical caryatids speak to the brilliant Hanging Lobster

Claw on the right, and the Fishbone Cactus on the left. This cactus rarely flowers, and when it does it blooms at night and lasts a day: the image is a photograph of one that burst unexpectedly into bloom when Hammond was visiting her sister. Serendipity is one of the joys of the found image – she cherishes printing mistakes and oddities – but so is meticulous craft.

The ground, like the vase, can dictate mood. At one point, hunting for an effect like the sixth-century gilt mosaics at San Vitale in Ravenna, Hammond cut and glued what seemed like a thousand tiny pieces, only to find that the gold fought with all the flowers she tried. Finally, in *French Glass with Emerald Cuckoo, Malachite Sunbird and Carmine Bee-eater* (2017), she solved the problem by making a monochrome arrangement of flowers and foliage, using subtle tones of black and white. The only colour here comes from the flashes of the birds that hover and perch on the curling branches. Behind them the gold mosaic has become mobile, rippling with light.

The collages are sublimely artificial, a chorus of botanical impossibilities. Playing with digital images, Hammond can reconfigure plants, alter colour and distort scale. The small Rafflesia arnoldii, such as the one that appears in *Top Hat Champagne Bucket with Hot Lips, Rafflesia and Button Medick* (2022), is actually the largest, heaviest flower in nature, up to a metre across. But even in its artfully dwarfed form, this vile-smelling 'corpse plant' looks like a fleshy beast, a sinister stranger. Witty details like this alert us to the liberties Hammond takes as an artist, but also to the oddities of nature itself. Evolution, she notes, outdoes art in invention, as in the use of mimicry to ward off predators or invite pollinating insects: a plant like the Monkeyface Orchid 'is almost a cartoon of itself'. Her works are a celebration, both of the variety of nature, and of the diversity of images. But they provoke thought as well as delight. When Hammond first saw Lynn Davis's stunning photographs of icebergs twenty years ago, she says, 'I thought, how wonderful – what must it have been like to be there? To be faced with these amazingly complex shapes that only she had seen? But now I look at those photographs differently. I first think – melting, global warming!' To find images of birds for the collages Hammond recalls, 'I used the internet like crazy.' When she looked up Indian kingfishers, she found hundreds of varieties; then came the Malaysian varieties, and the Indonesian… thousands of glorious creatures. But, she asks, 'in fifty years, where will all this plenitude be?' The abundance of forms in paintings of nature has always conjured a kind of Eden. With a new urgency, her luminous collages, with their striking blend of harmony and unsettling tension, return to the double theme of the earliest flower painting, the beauty and evanescence of nature and the power of art to preserve it, to hold its rich images through time.

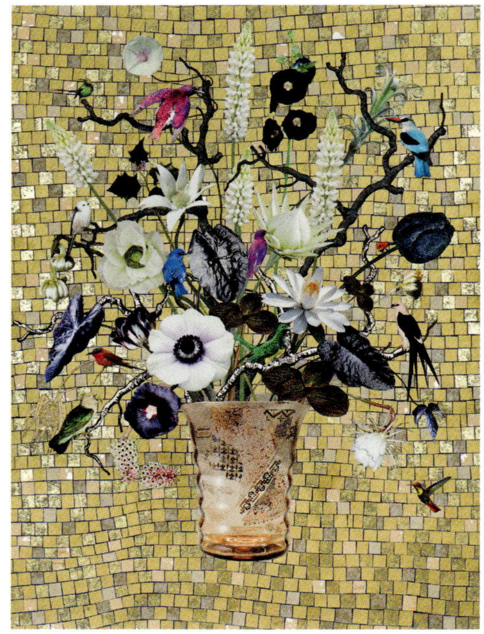

***French Glass with Emerald Cuckoo, Malachite Sunbird and Carmine Bee-eater*, 2017**
Unique botanical collage using lithography, linocut, relief printing, digital printing, coloured pencil, Sumi ink, watercolour and gouache, hand cut and assembled on a mosaic of various collaged gold papers over painted cotton rag
127 × 96.5 cm
50 × 38 in

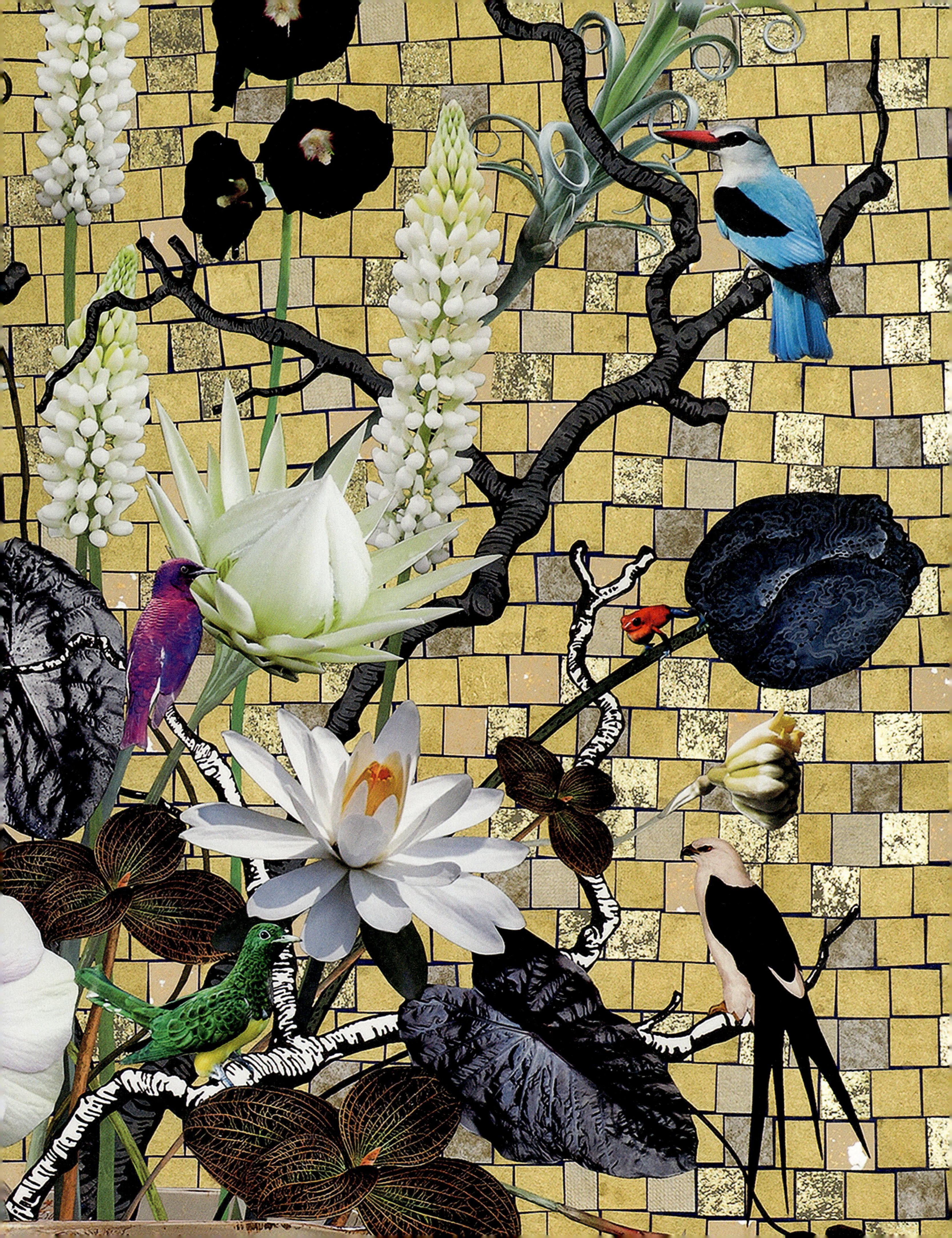

Champagne Bucket with Mouse Melons, Huitlacoche and Texas Black Sorghum, 2022
Unique botanical collage using linocut, digital printing, coloured pencil, Sumi ink, watercolour and gouache, hand cut and assembled on collaged Japanese and Thai papers over painted cotton rag
127 × 96.5 cm
50 × 38 in

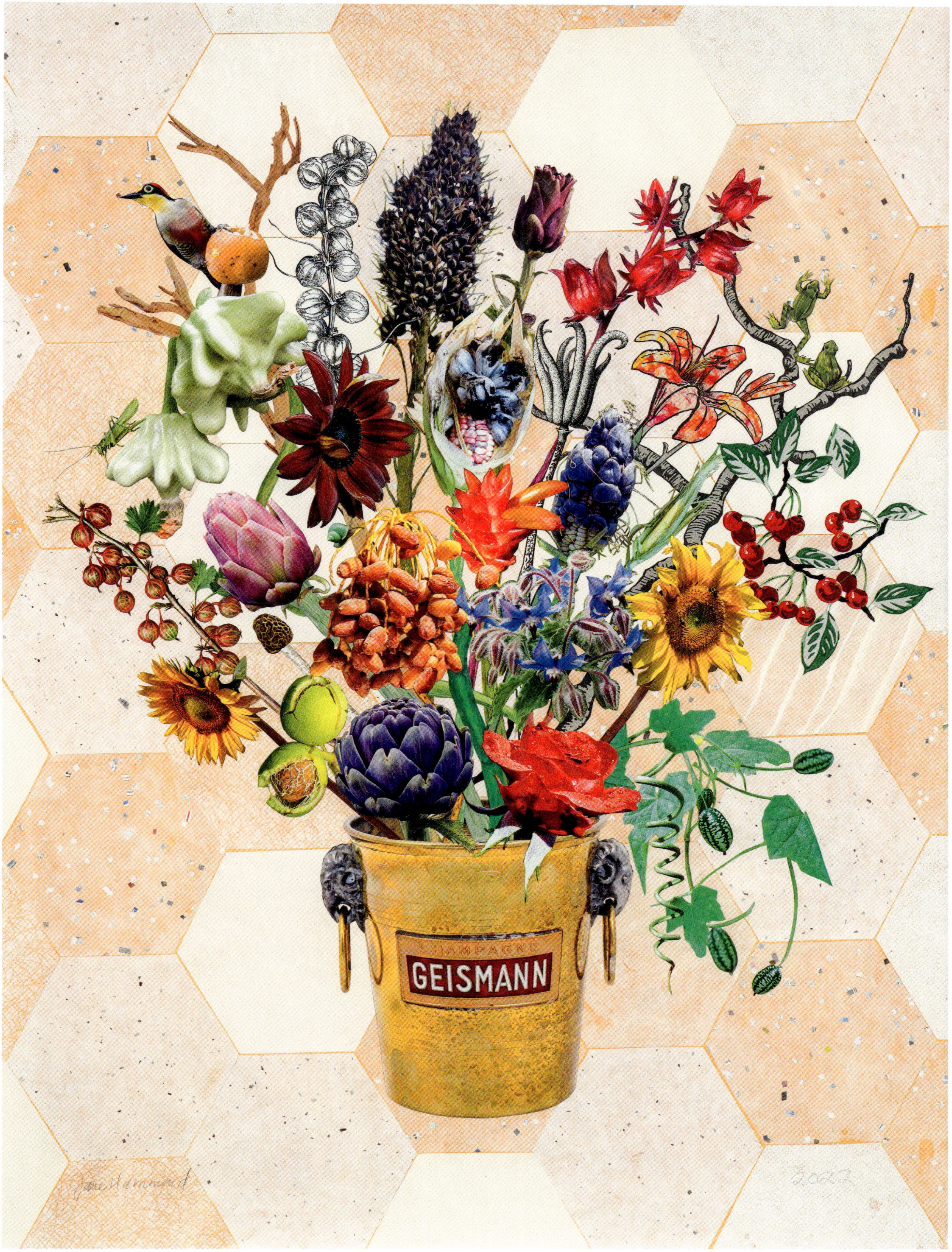
CHAMPAGNE
GEISMANN
2022

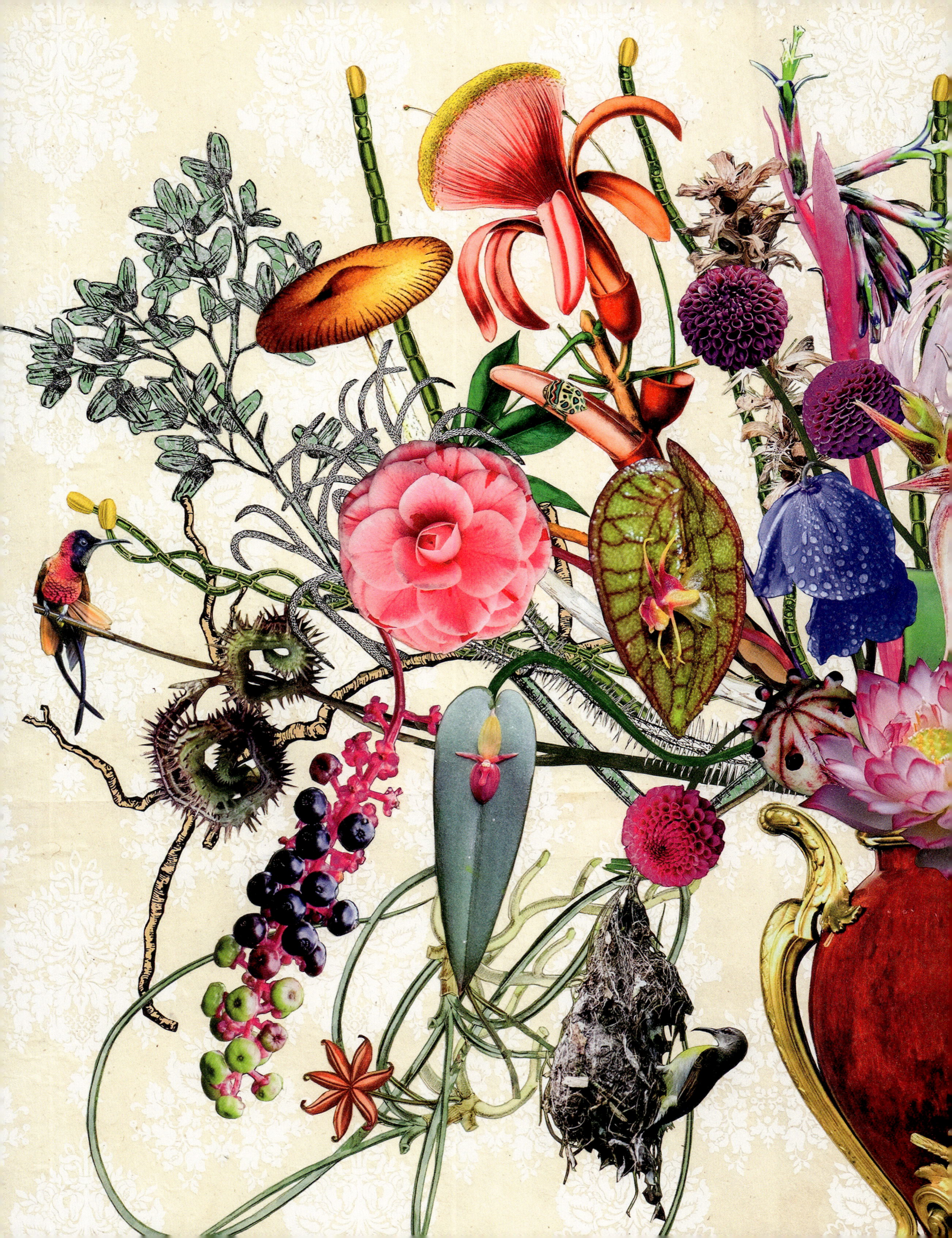

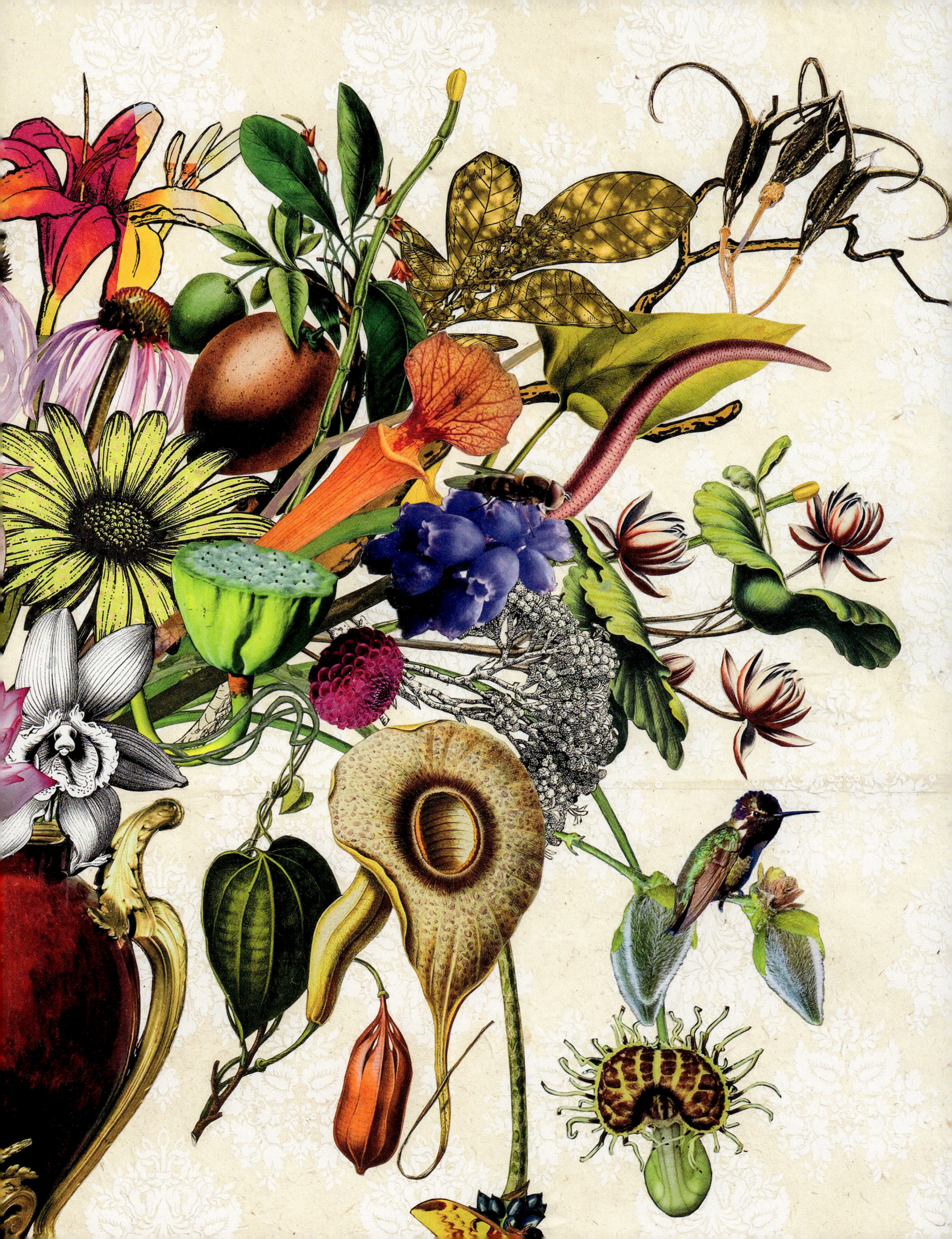

French Sang de Boeuf and Gilt Bronze Centerpiece with Camellia, Crimson Topaz and Pokeberries, 2025
Unique botanical collage using relief printing, linocut, digital printing, coloured pencil, Sumi ink, watercolour and gouache, hand cut and assembled on collaged Nepali papers over cotton rag
96.5 × 127 cm
38 × 50 in

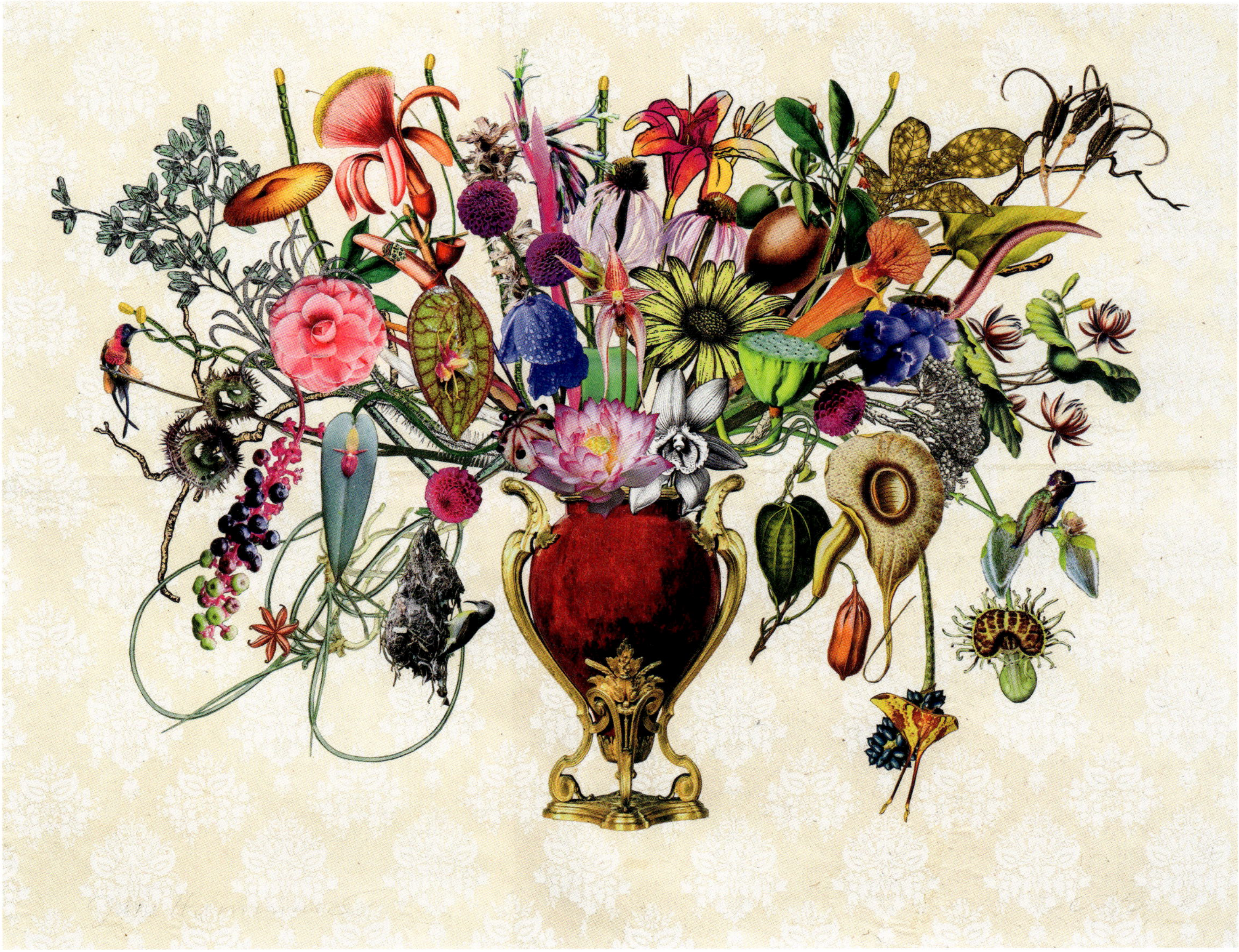

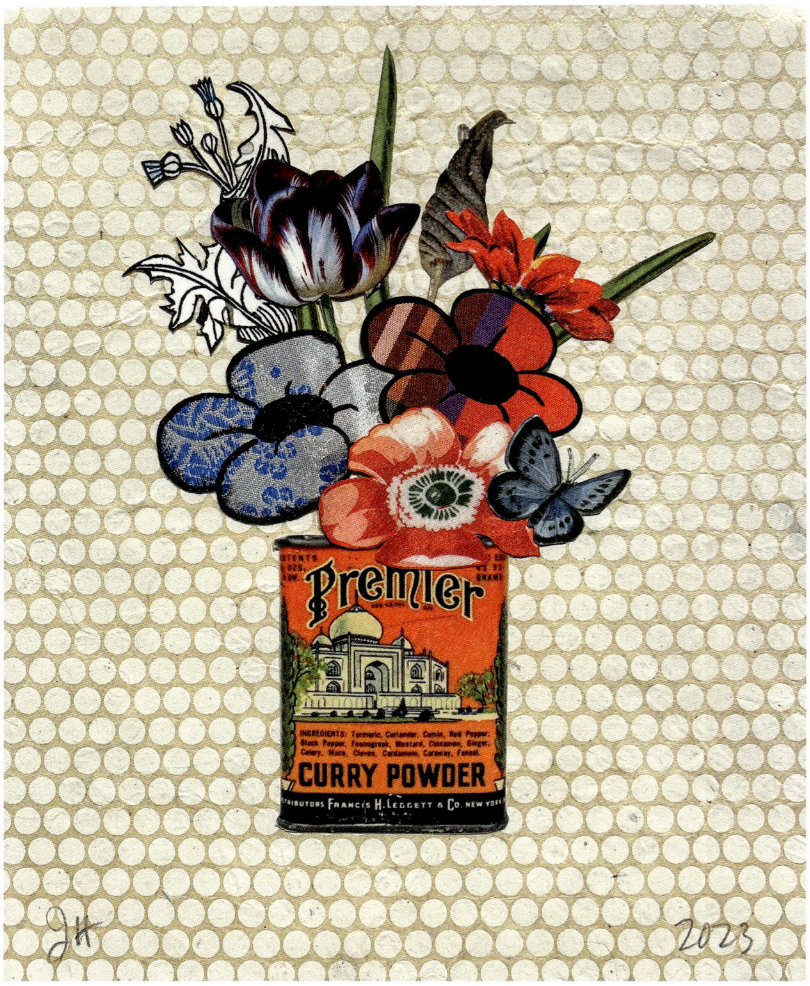

Premium Curry with Poppy and Tulip, 2025
Unique botanical collage using digital printing, coloured pencil, Sumi ink, watercolour, gouache and brocade fabric, hand cut and assembled on collaged Nepali paper over cotton rag
24.8 × 20.3 cm
9¾ × 8 in

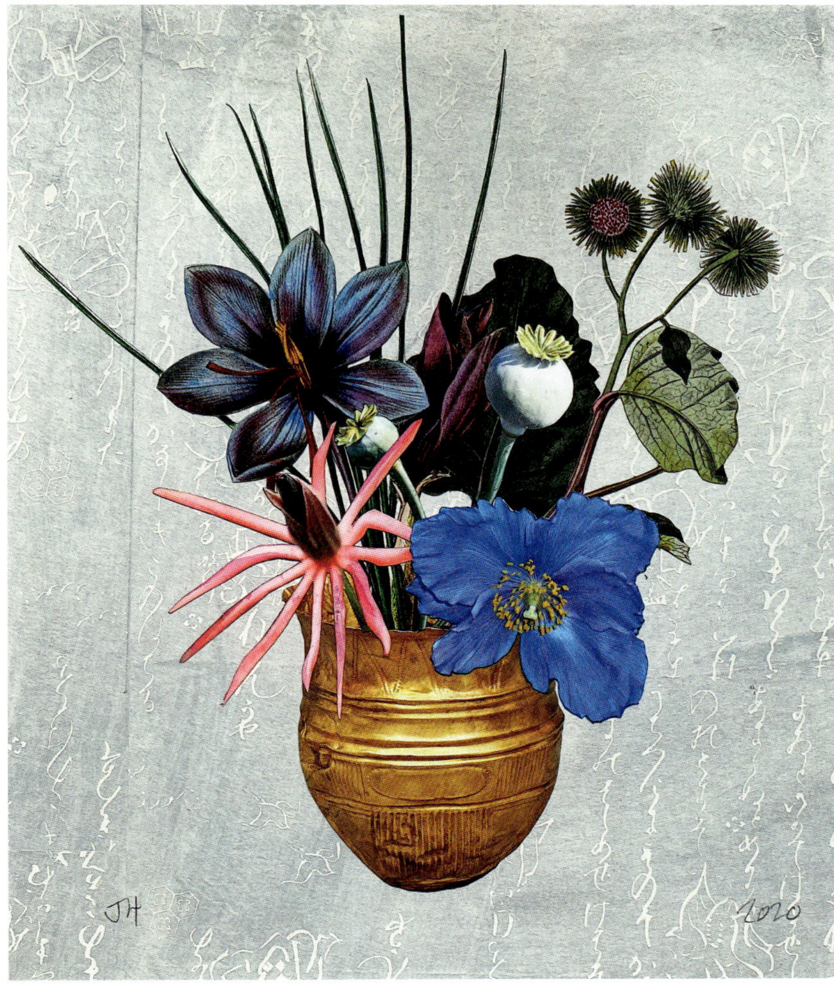

Bronze Age Gold Cup with Meconopsis and Burrs, 2020
Unique botanical collage with digital printing, watercolour and gouache, hand cut and assembled on collaged Japanese papers over painted cotton rag
32.4 × 27.9 cm
12¾ × 11 in

San Francisco Yacht Club Trophy with Paradise Flycatcher, Nigella and Xerces Blues, 2023
Unique botanical collage using digital printing, coloured pencil, Sumi ink, watercolour and gouache, hand cut and assembled on collaged Japanese papers over painted cotton rag
106.7 × 88.9 cm
42 × 35 in

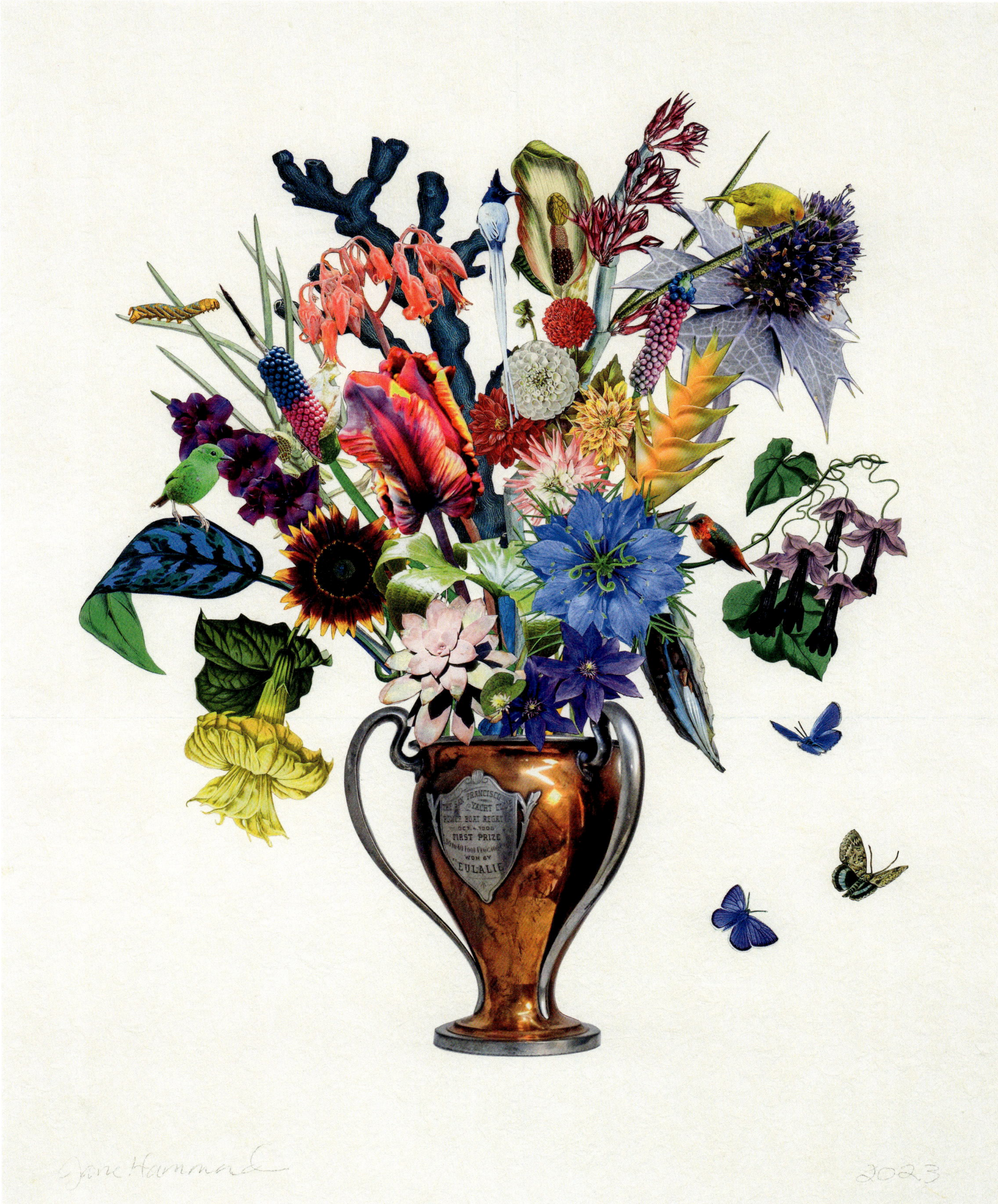
FIRST PRIZE
EULALIE
2023

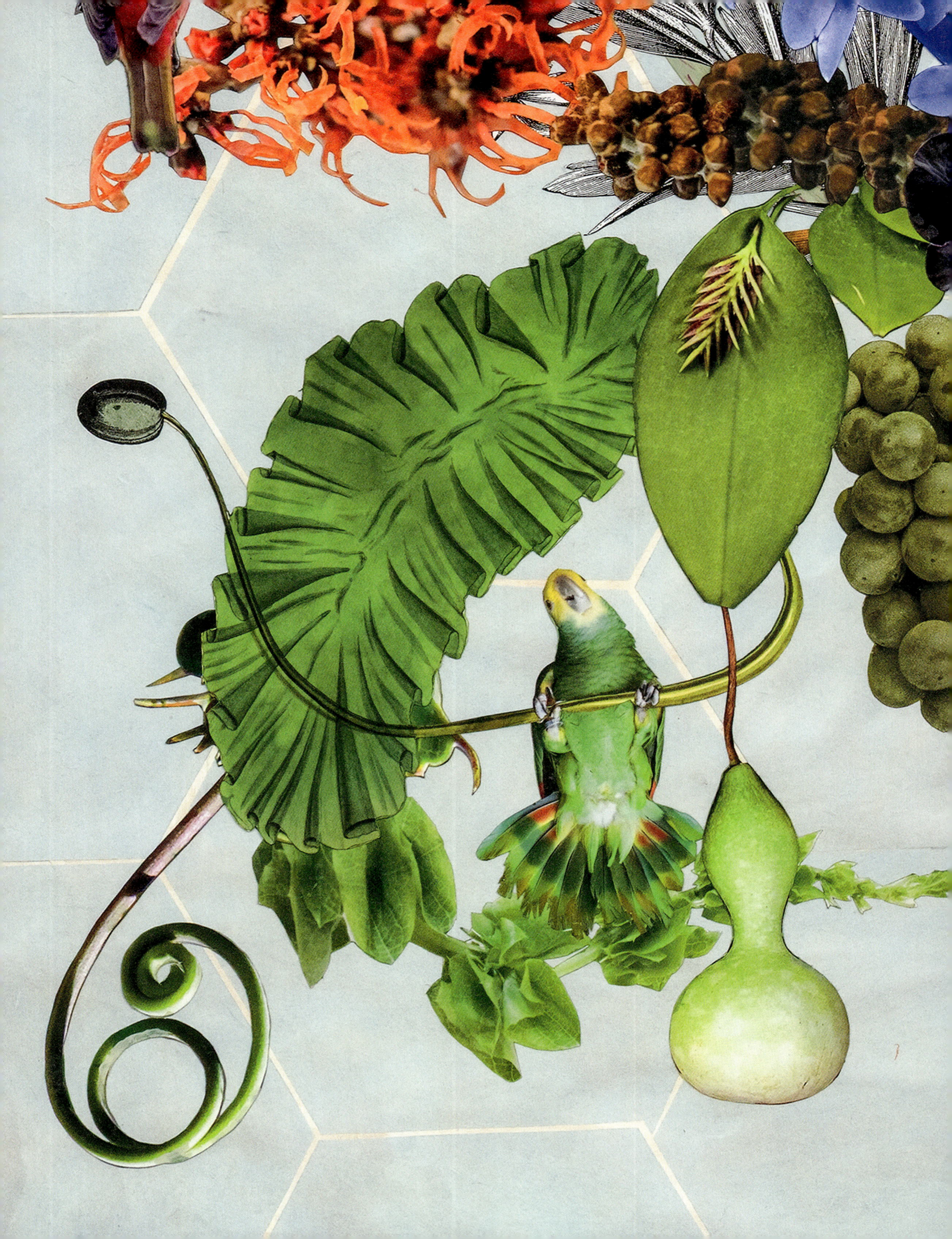

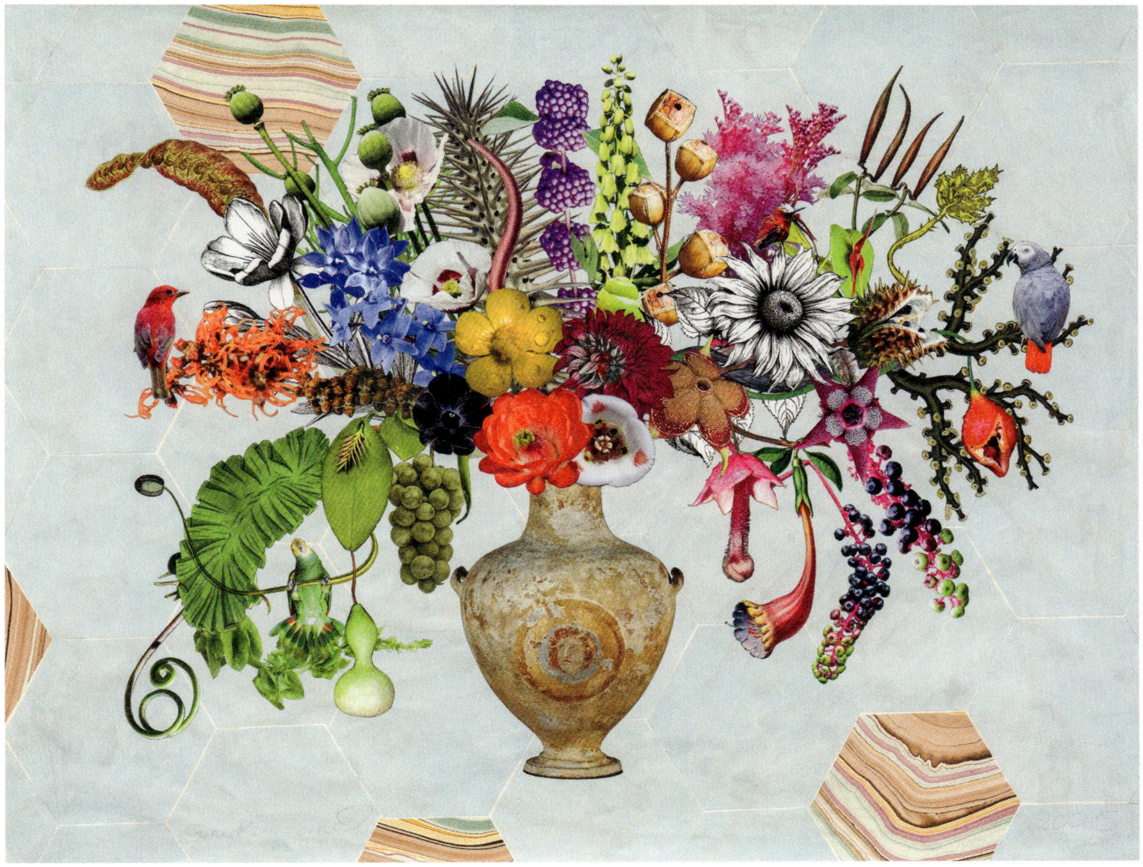

Ancient Greek Hydra with Witch Hazel, Buttercup and African Grey Parrot, 2025
Unique botanical collage using relief printing, digital printing, coloured pencil, Sumi ink, watercolour and gouache, hand cut and assembled on collaged Japanese and Italian papers over painted cotton rag
96.5 × 127 cm
38 × 50 in

Korean Buncheong Vase with Monkshood, Jack-in-the-Pulpit and White Sunflowers, 2024
Unique botanical collage using relief printing, digital printing, coloured pencil, Sumi ink, watercolour and gouache, hand cut and assembled on collaged Nepali and Japanese papers over cotton rag
127 × 96.5 cm
50 × 38 in

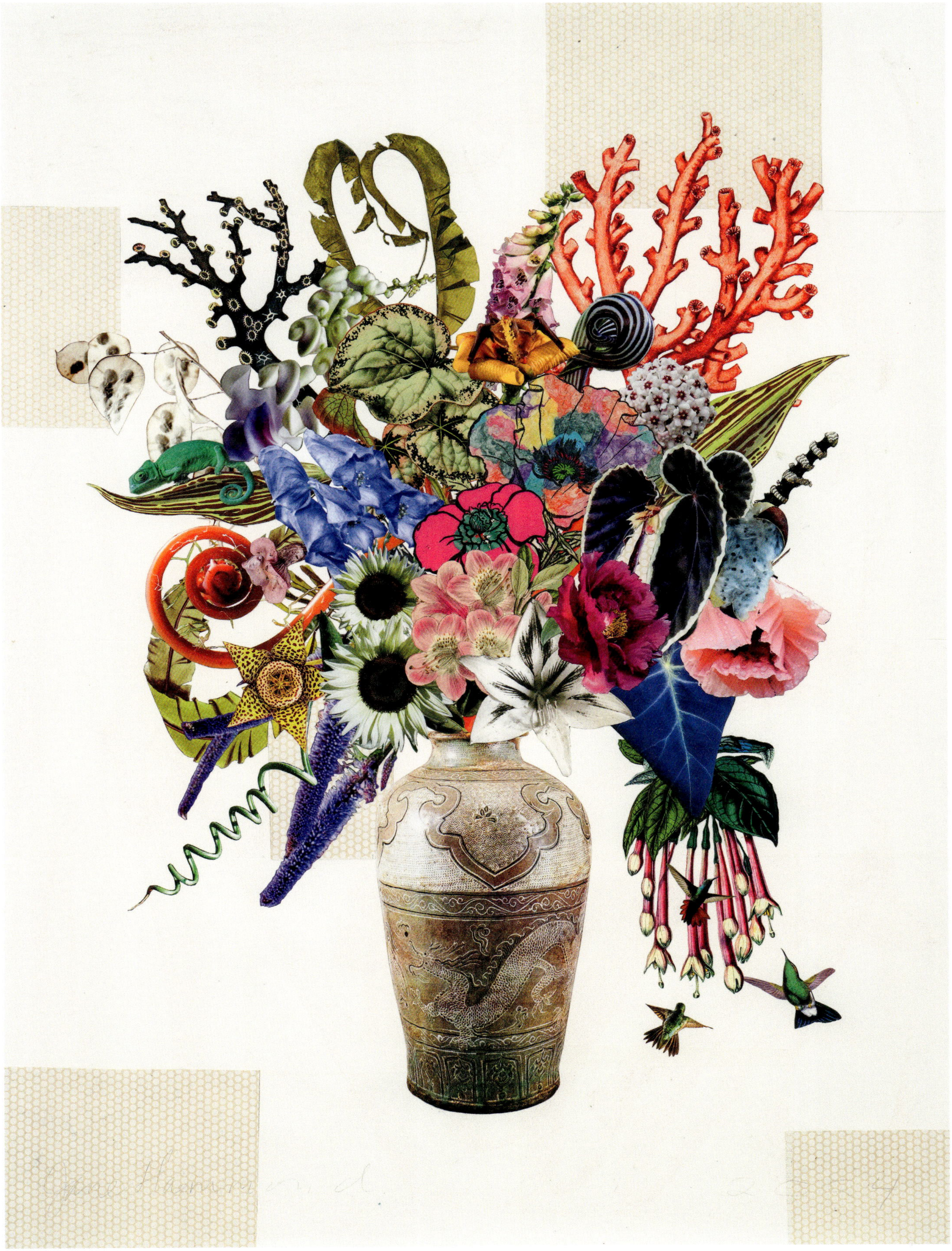

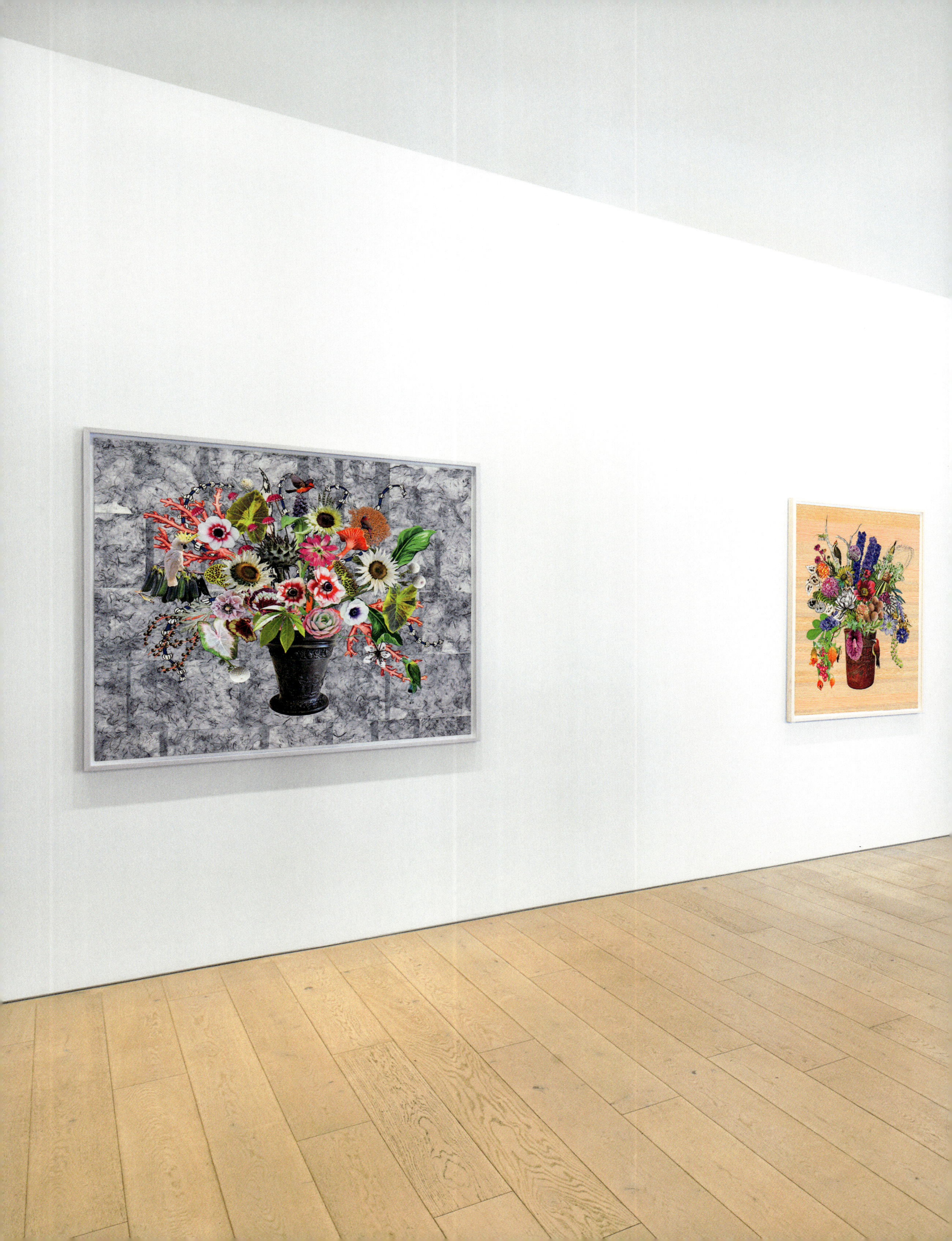

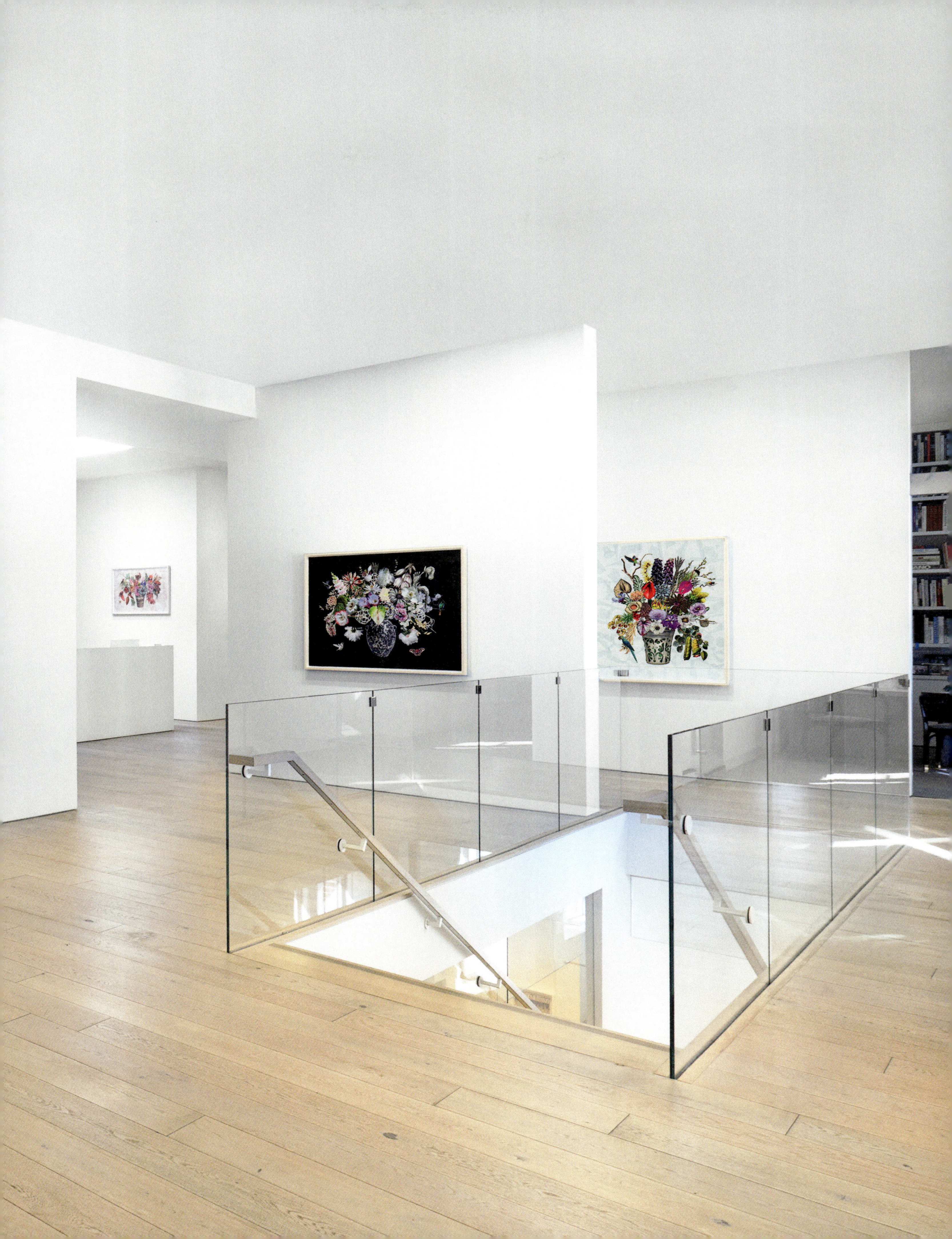

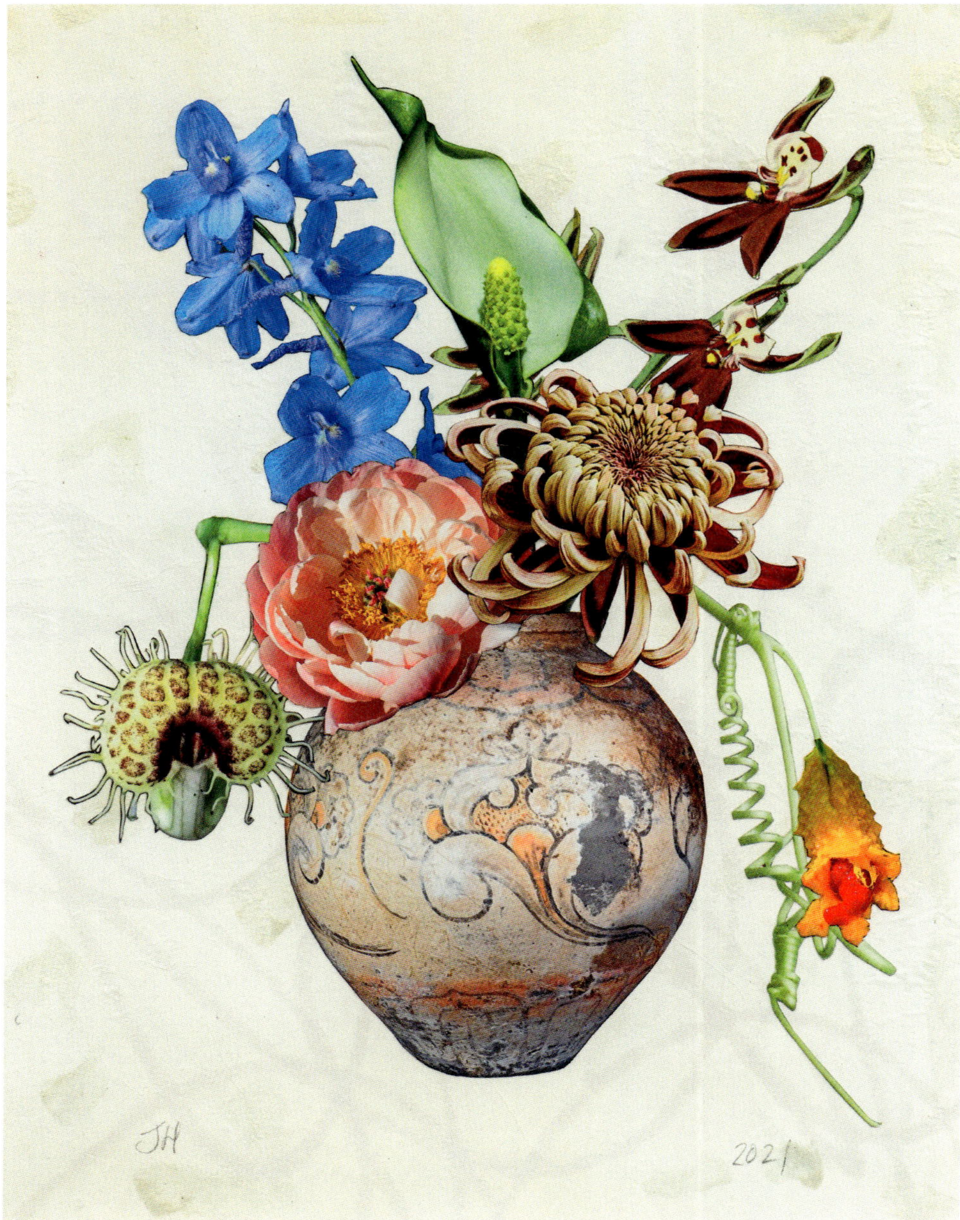

Chinese Painted Vase with Delphinium, Momordica and Chrysanthemum, 2021
Unique botanical collage with digital printing, coloured pencil, Sumi ink, watercolour and gouache, hand cut and assembled on Japanese paper over cotton rag
45.1 × 35.6 cm
17¾ × 14 in

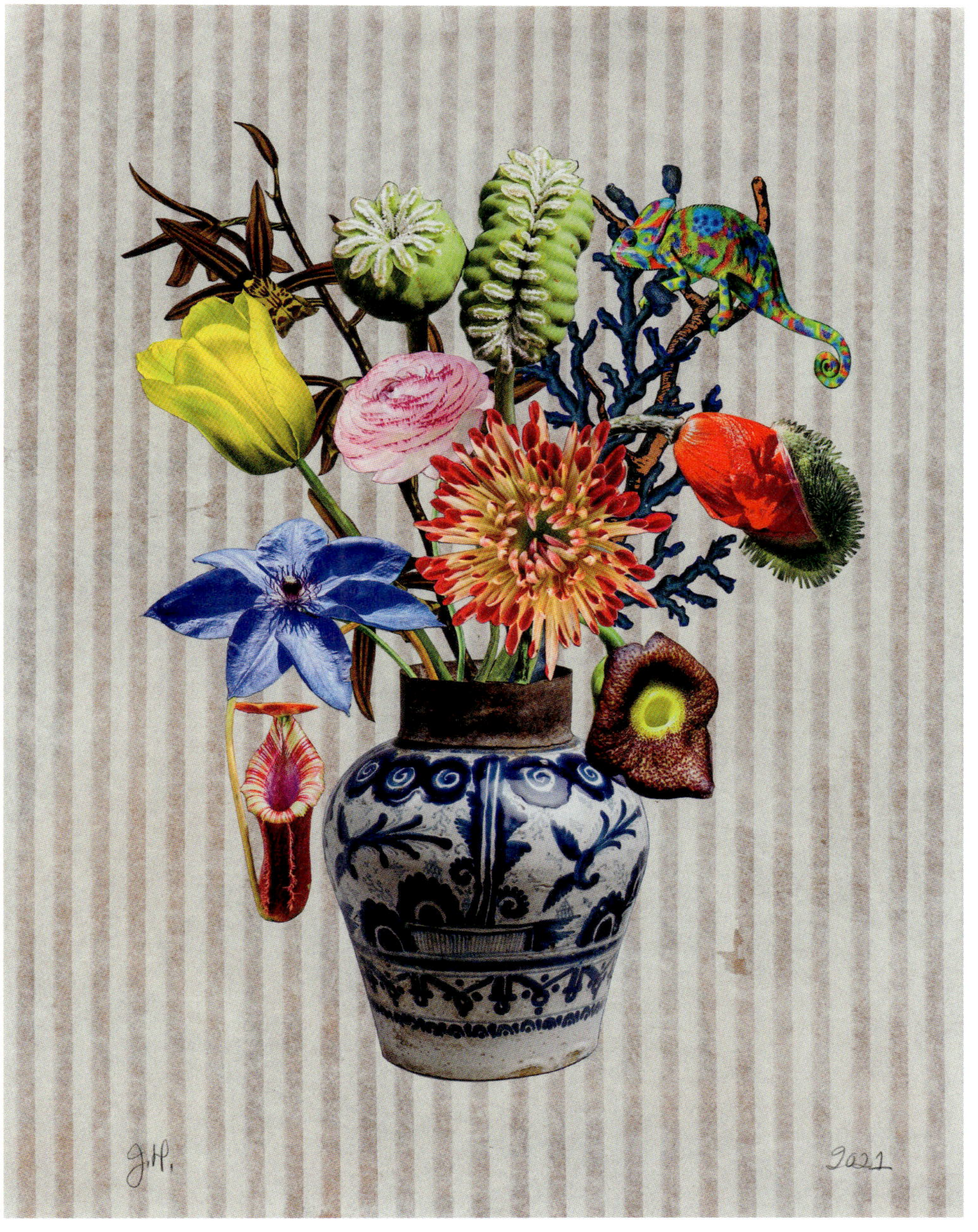

Mexican Chocolate Jar with Poppy Pods,
Pitcher Plant and Chameleon, 2021
Unique botanical collage with linocut, digital printing, coloured pencil, Sumi ink, watercolour and gouache, hand cut and assembled on Japanese paper over painted cotton rag
66 × 52.1 cm
26 × 20½ in

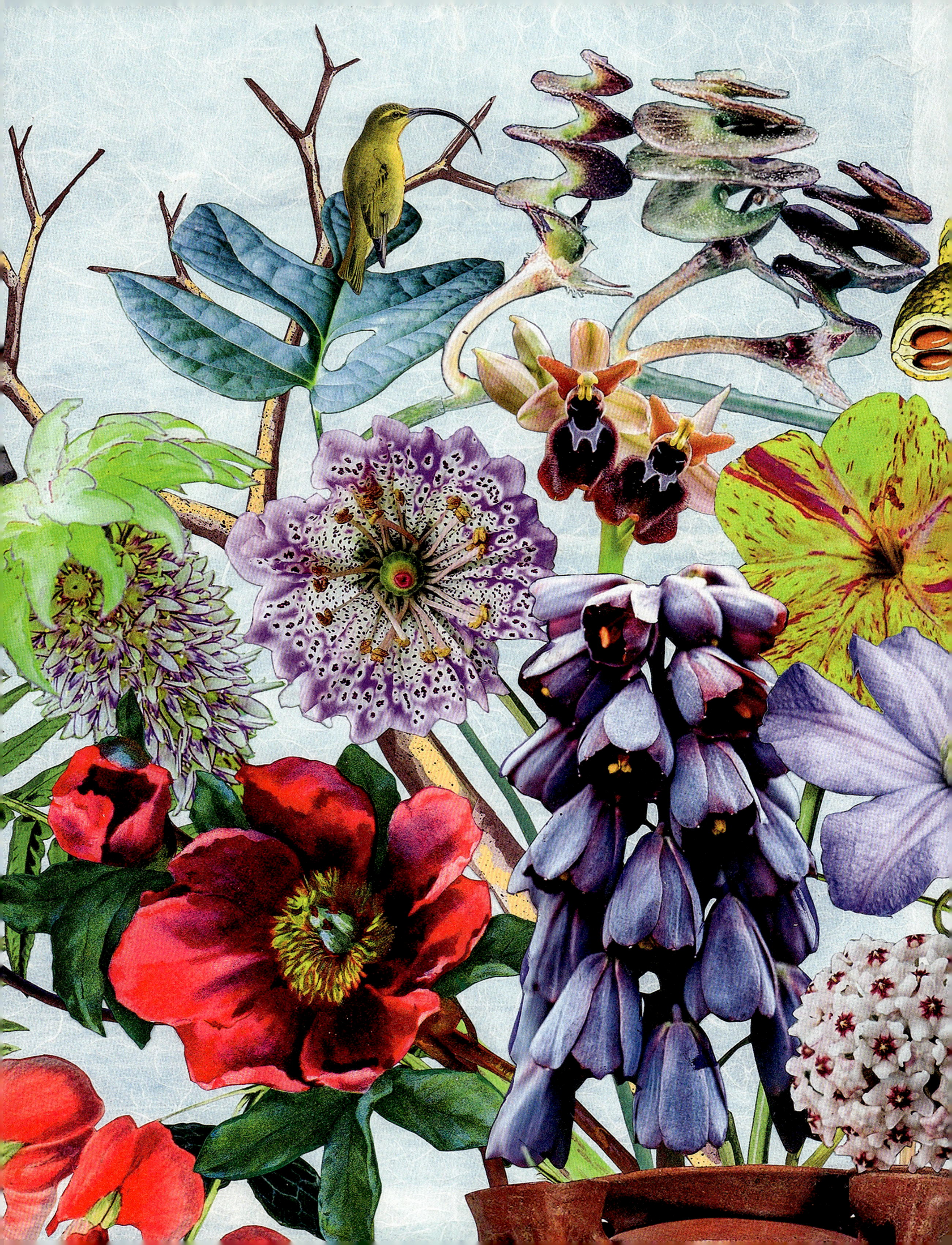

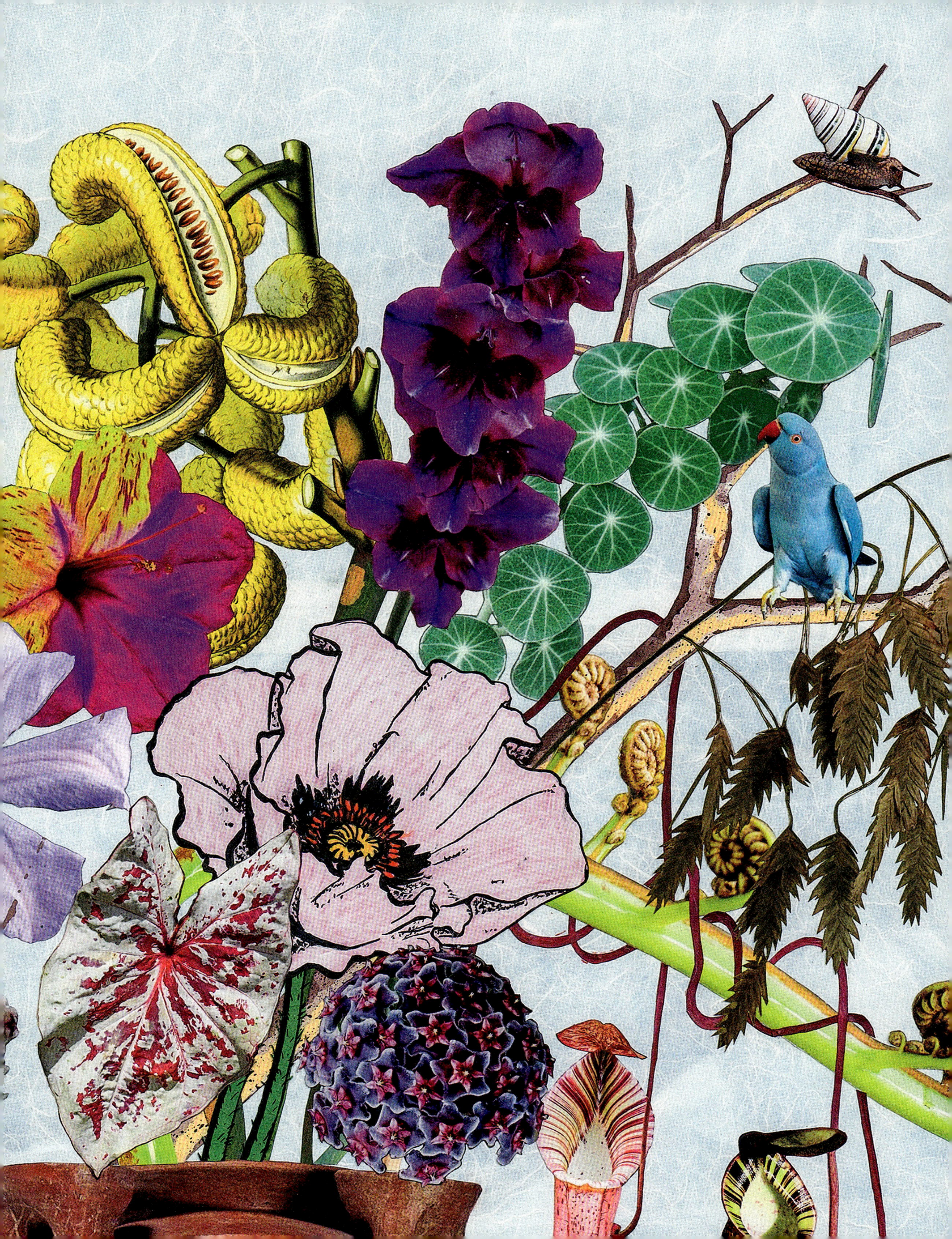

Etruscan Kernos with Guianan Trogon, Four O'Clocks and Pineapple Lily, 2023
Unique botanical collage using relief printing, digital printing, coloured pencil, Sumi ink, watercolour and gouache, hand cut and assembled on collaged Japanese papers over painted cotton rag
96.5 × 127 cm
38 × 50 in

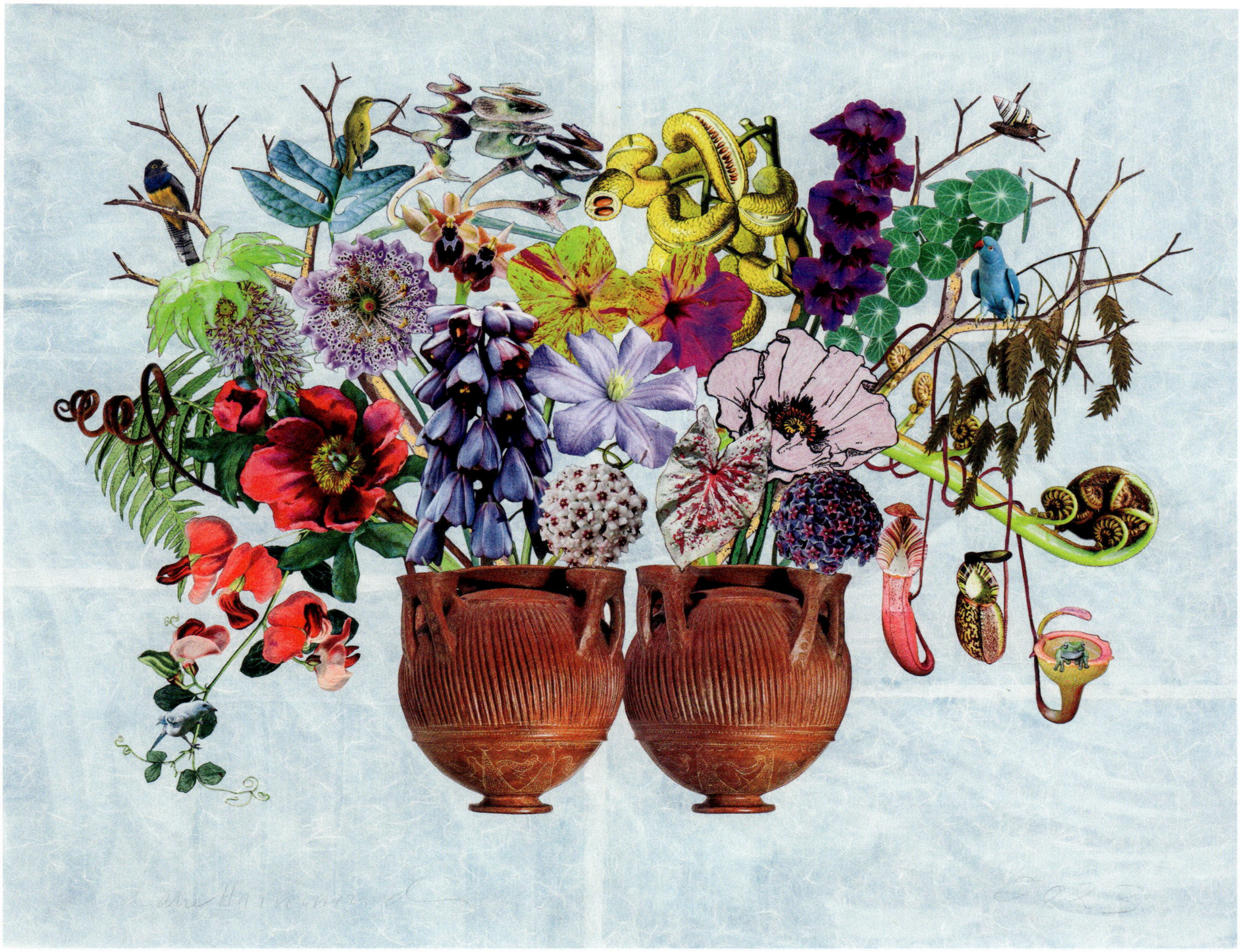

Francois Rousseau Vase with Swaddled Babies, Flaming Sword and Bells of Ireland, 2022
Unique botanical collage using linocut, relief printing, digital printing, coloured pencil, Sumi ink, watercolour, gouache and Mylar, hand cut and assembled on collaged Japanese papers over cotton rag
127 × 96.5 cm
50 × 38 in

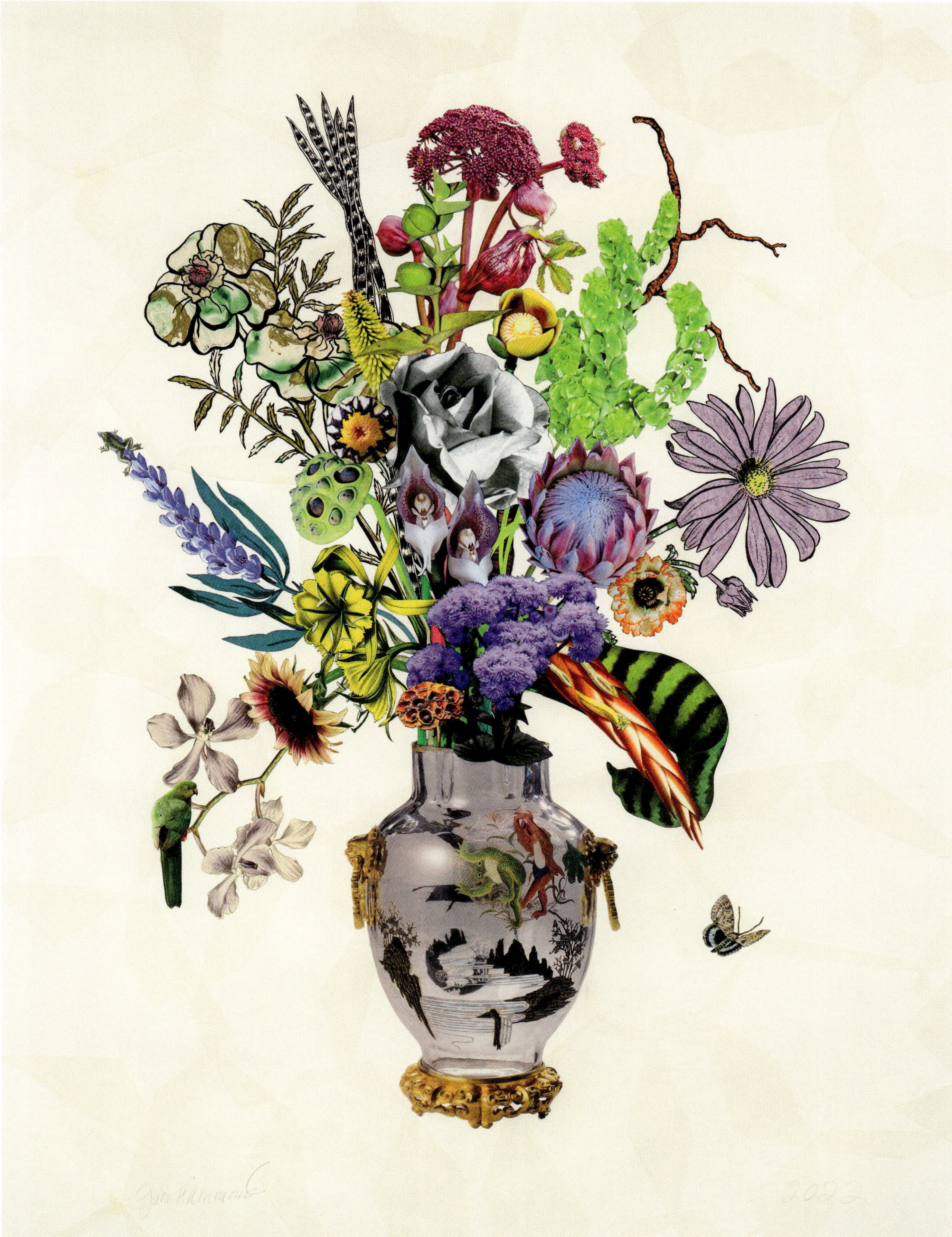

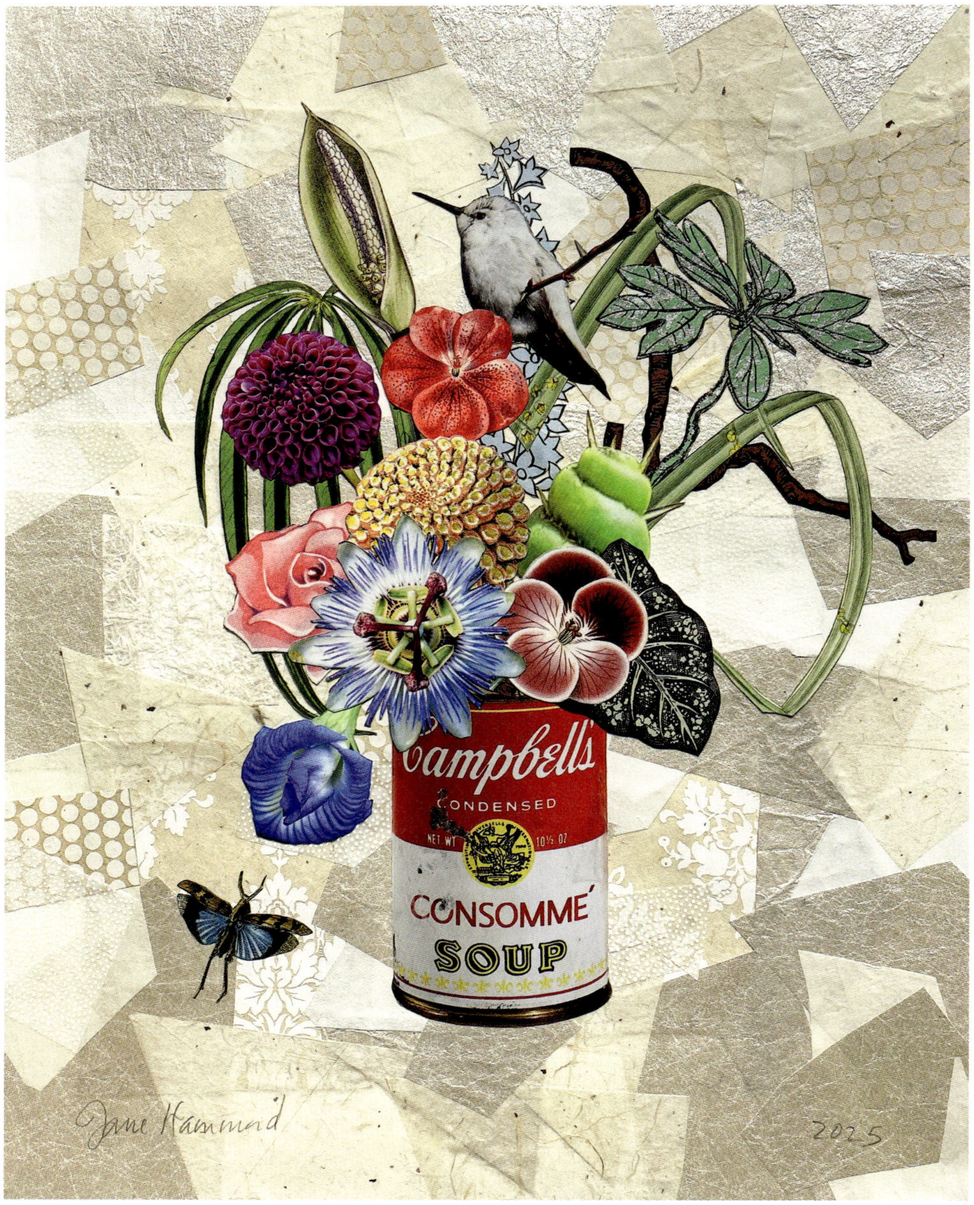

Campbell's Consomme with Passion Flower, Dahlia and Butterfly Pea, 2025
Unique botanical collage using relief printing, linocut, digital printing, coloured pencil, Sumi ink, watercolour and gouache, hand cut and assembled on collaged Japanese and Nepali papers over cotton rag
45.7 × 36.8 cm
18 × 14½ in

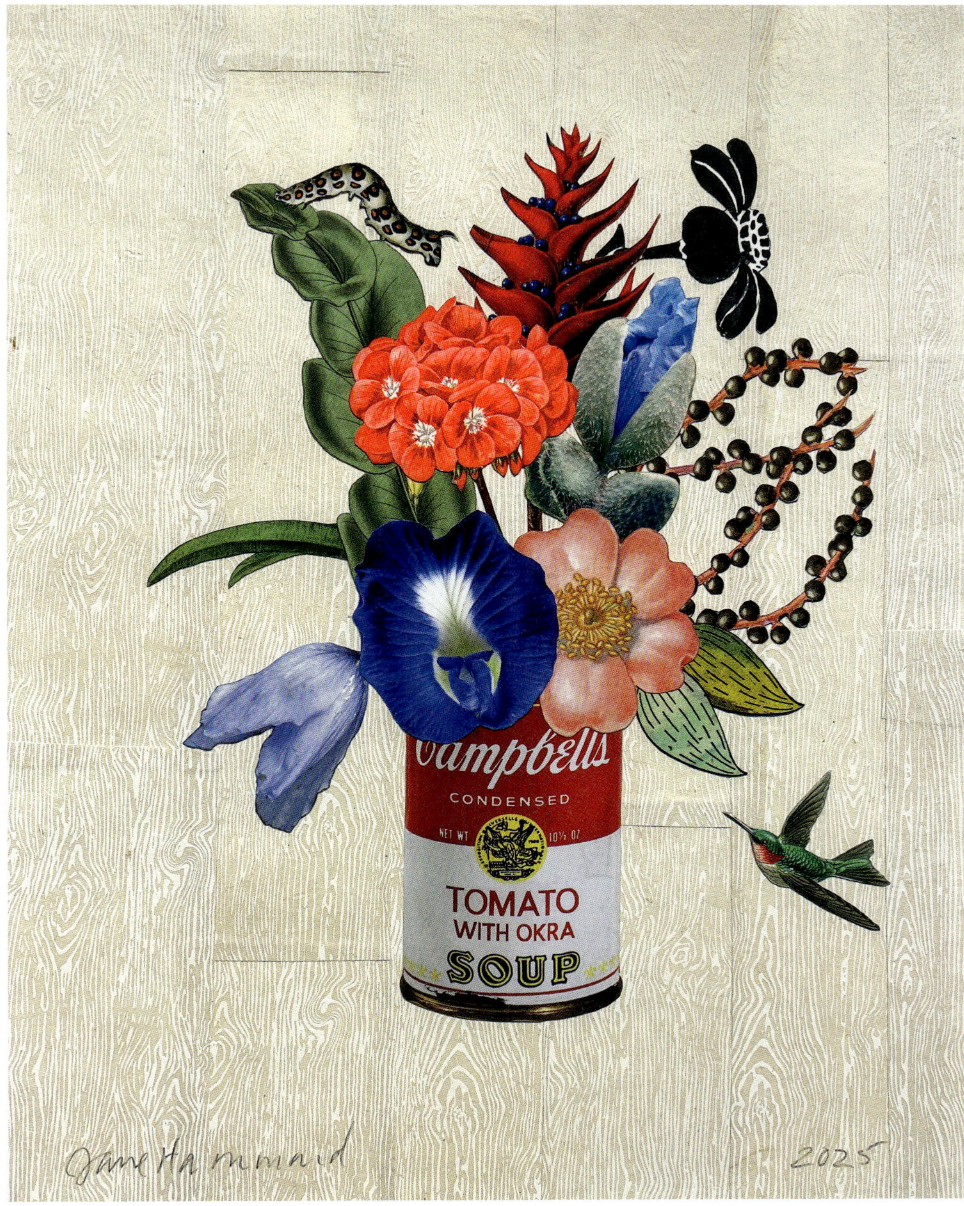

Campbell's Tomato with Okra with Geranium, Leopard Worm and Butterfly Pea, 2025
Unique botanical collage using relief printing, digital printing, coloured pencil, watercolour and gouache, hand cut and assembled on collaged Nepali papers over cotton rag
45.7 × 36.8 cm
18 × 14½ in

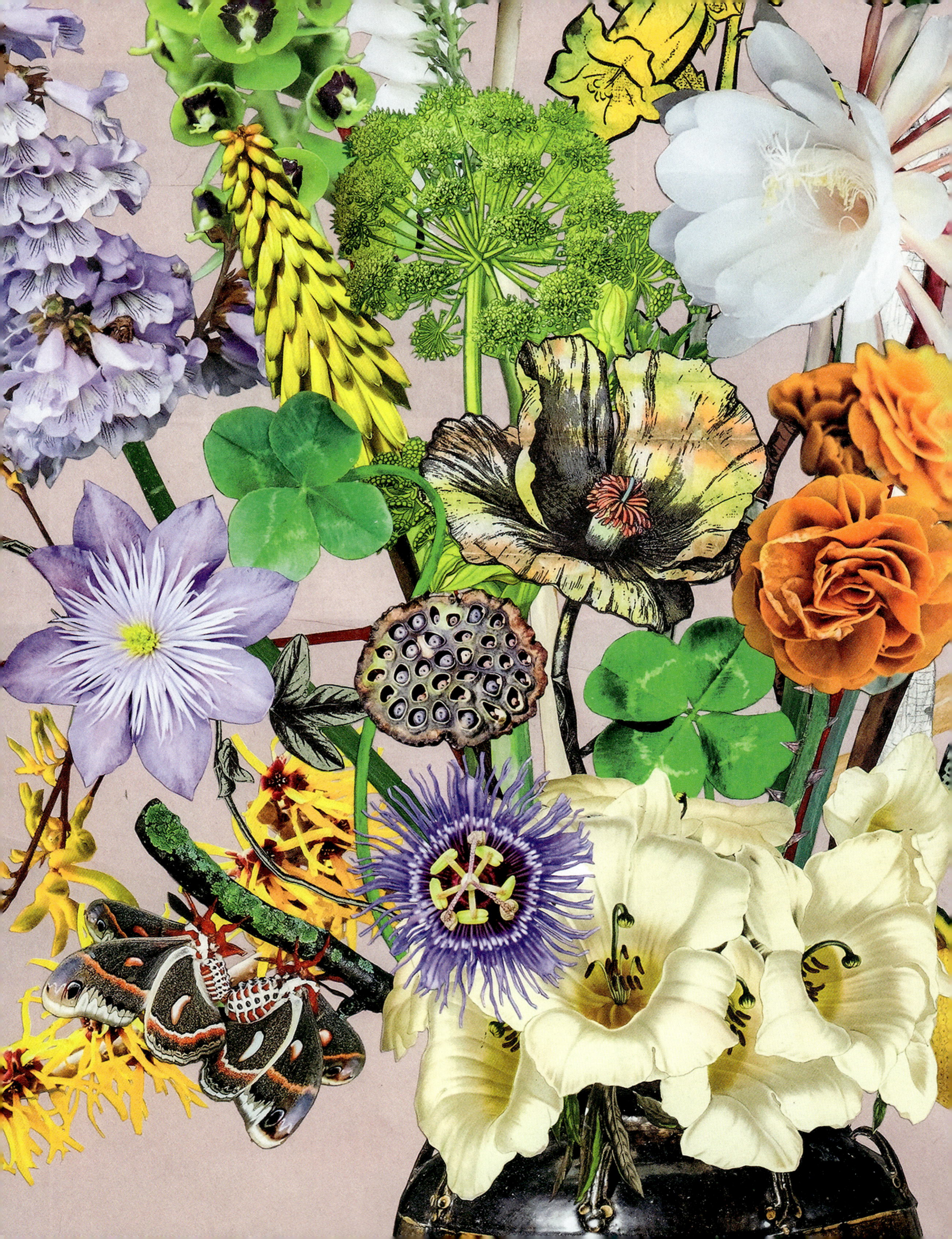

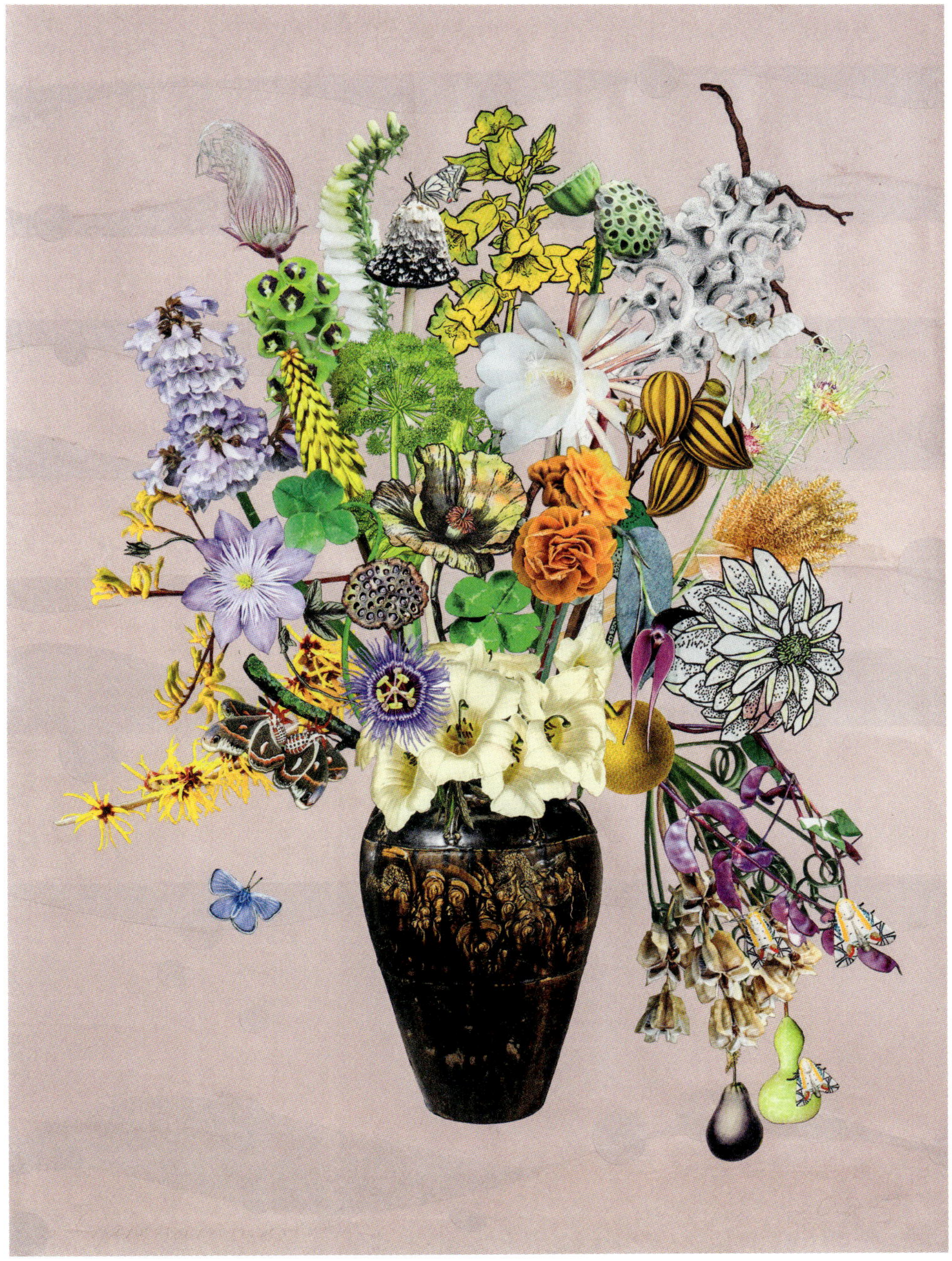

Martaban Jar with Prairie Smoke, Witch Hazel and Three Picasso Moths, 2025
Unique botanical collage using relief printing, linocut, digital printing, coloured pencil, Sumi ink, watercolour and gouache, hand cut and assembled on collaged Japanese papers over cotton rag
127 × 96.5 cm
50 × 38 in

French Deco Vase with Elephant-Foot Yam, Medinilla Magnifica and Four Black-and-Yellow Broadbills, 2023
Unique botanical collage using digital printing, coloured pencil, Sumi ink, watercolour and gouache, hand cut and assembled on collaged Japanese, Thai and Nepali papers over painted cotton rag
127 × 96.5 cm
50 × 38 in

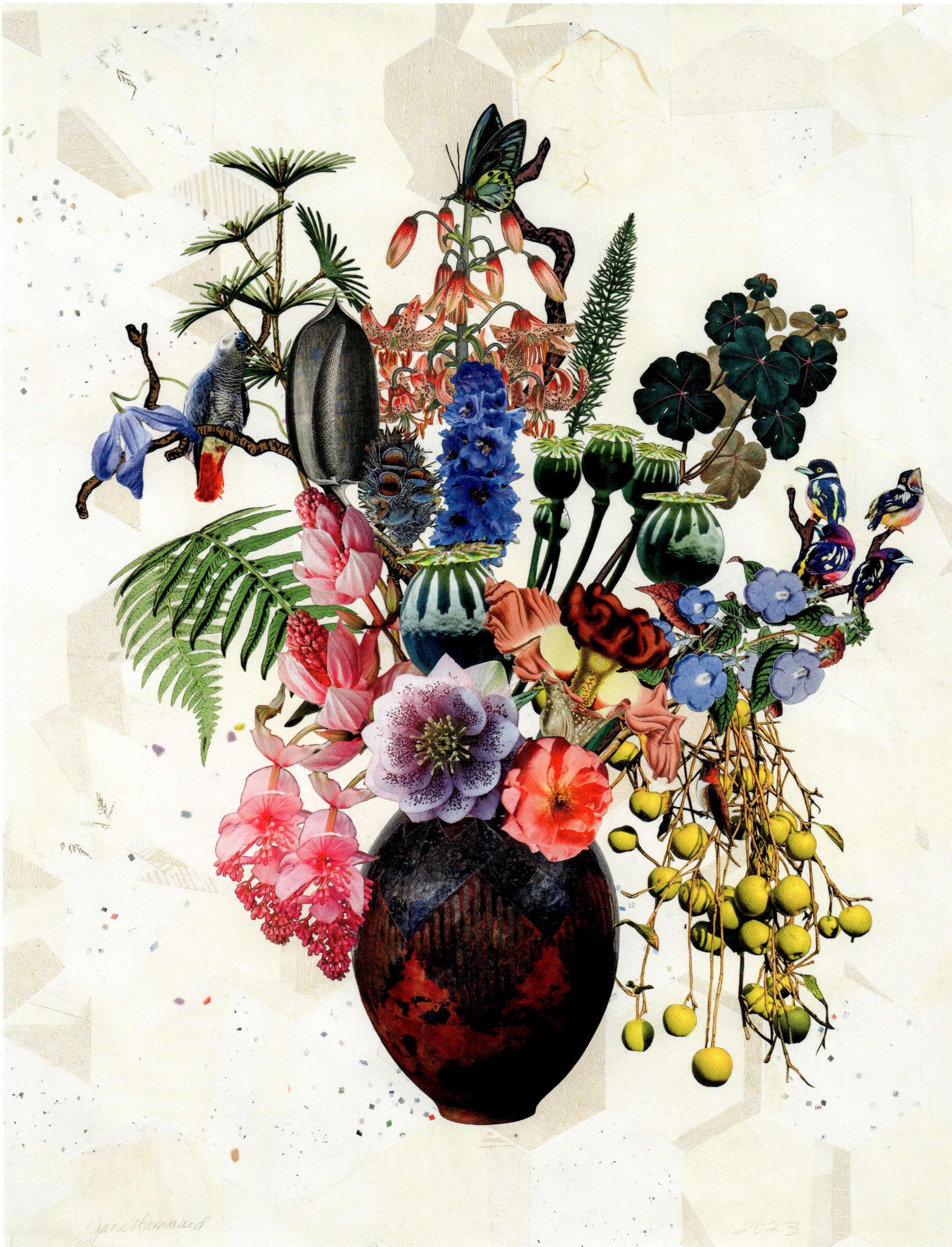

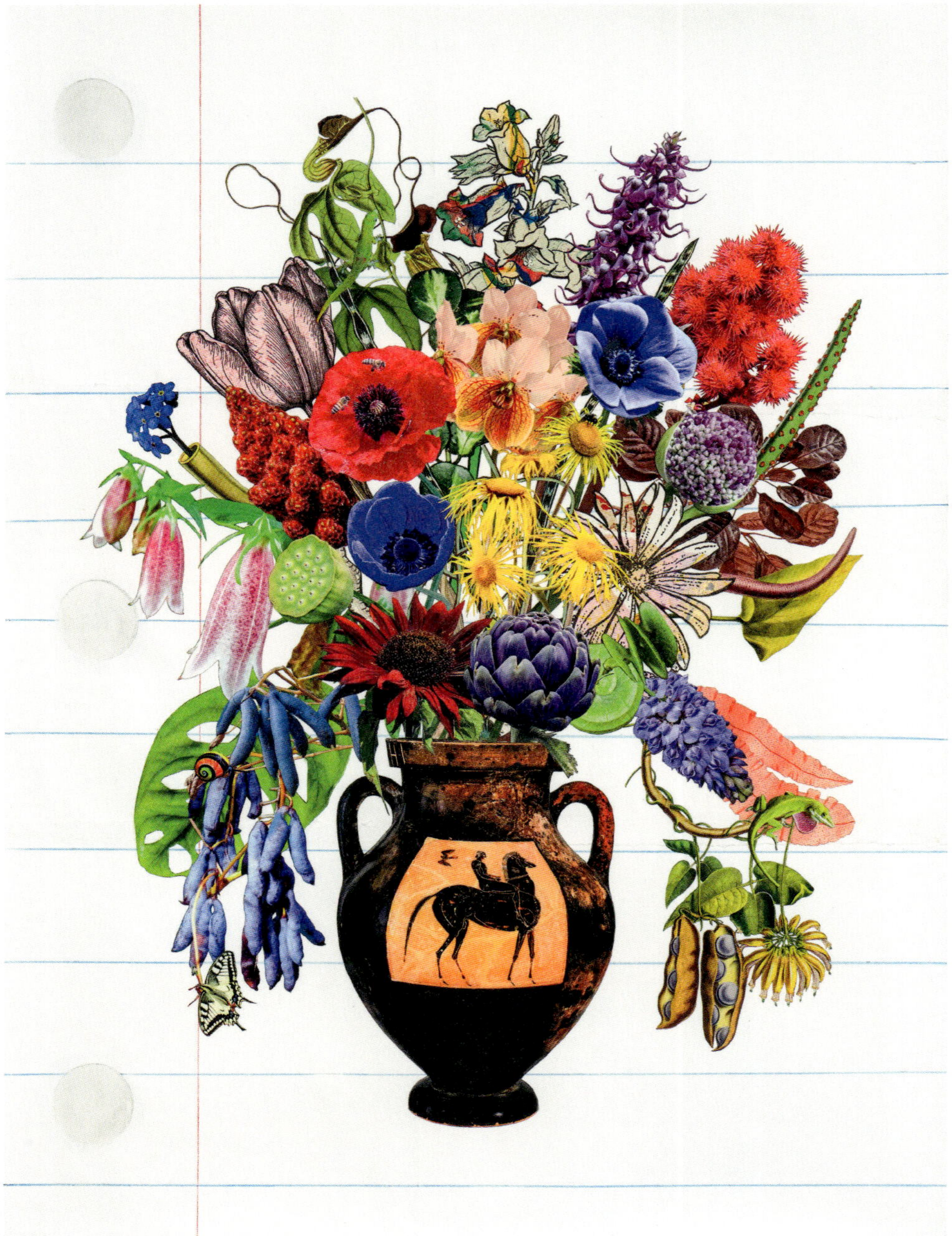

Greek Equestrian Amphora with Anemones, Elephant Head Orchid and Bull's Eye Beans, 2025
Unique botanical collage using relief printing, linocut, digital printing, coloured pencil, Sumi ink, watercolour and gouache, hand cut and assembled on collaged Japanese papers over painted cotton rag
127 × 96.5 cm
50 × 38 in

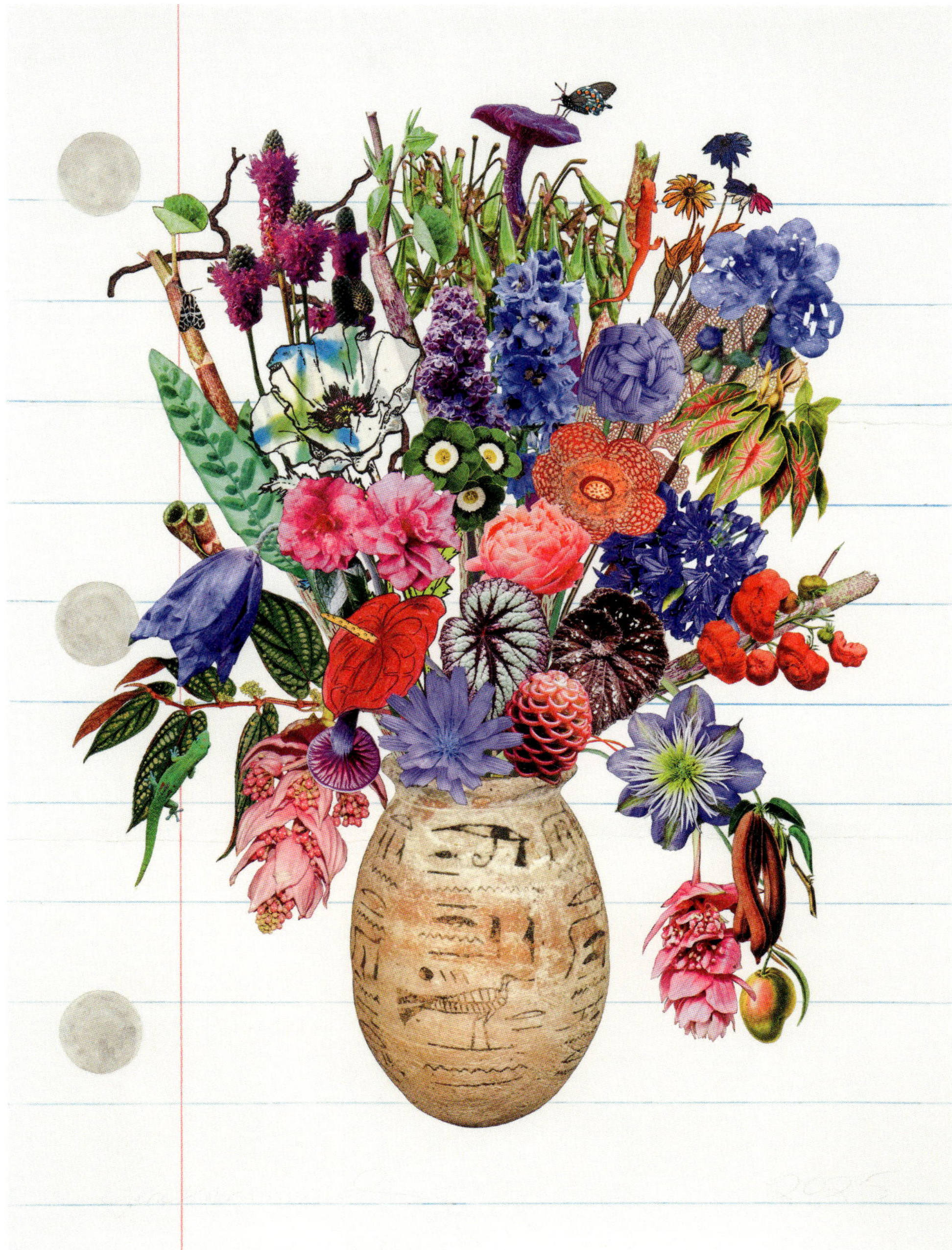

***Egyptian Vase with Sow Thistle, Amethyst Deceiver and Himalayan Balsam*, 2025**
Unique botanical collage using relief printing, linocut, digital printing, coloured pencil, Sumi ink, watercolour and gouache, hand cut and assembled on collaged Japanese papers over painted cotton rag
127 × 96.5 cm
50 × 38 in

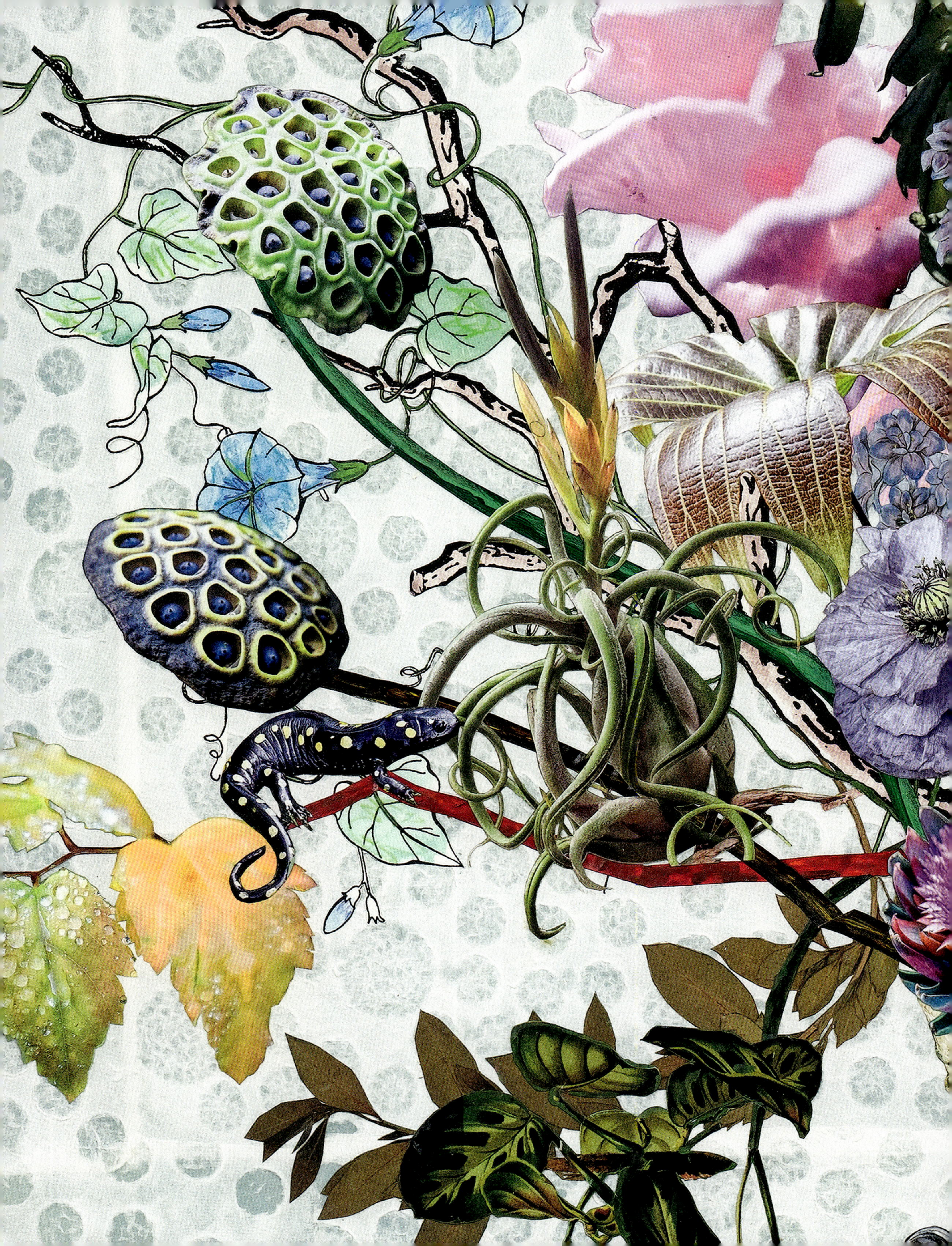

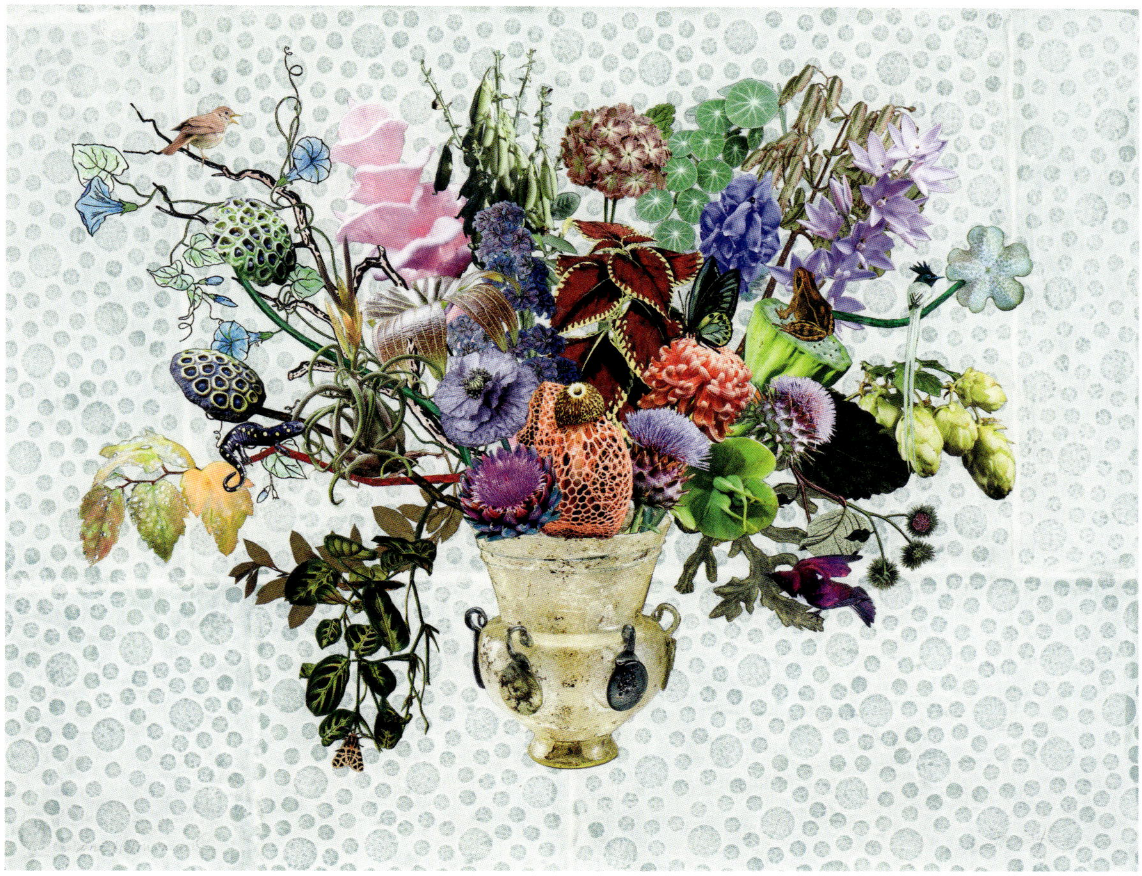

Mosque Lamp with Nightingale, Cardoons and Leopard Frog, 2024
Unique botanical collage with relief print, digital printing, coloured pencil, Sumi ink, watercolour and gouache, hand cut and assembled on collaged Thai papers over painted cotton rag
96.5 × 127 cm
38 × 50 in

Syrian Silver and Copper Vase with Shaggy Scarlet Cups, Pears and Lotus Leaves, 2024
Unique botanical collage with relief print, digital printing, coloured pencil, Sumi ink, watercolour and gouache, hand cut and assembled on collaged Nepali papers over painted cotton rag
127 × 96.5 cm
50 × 38 in

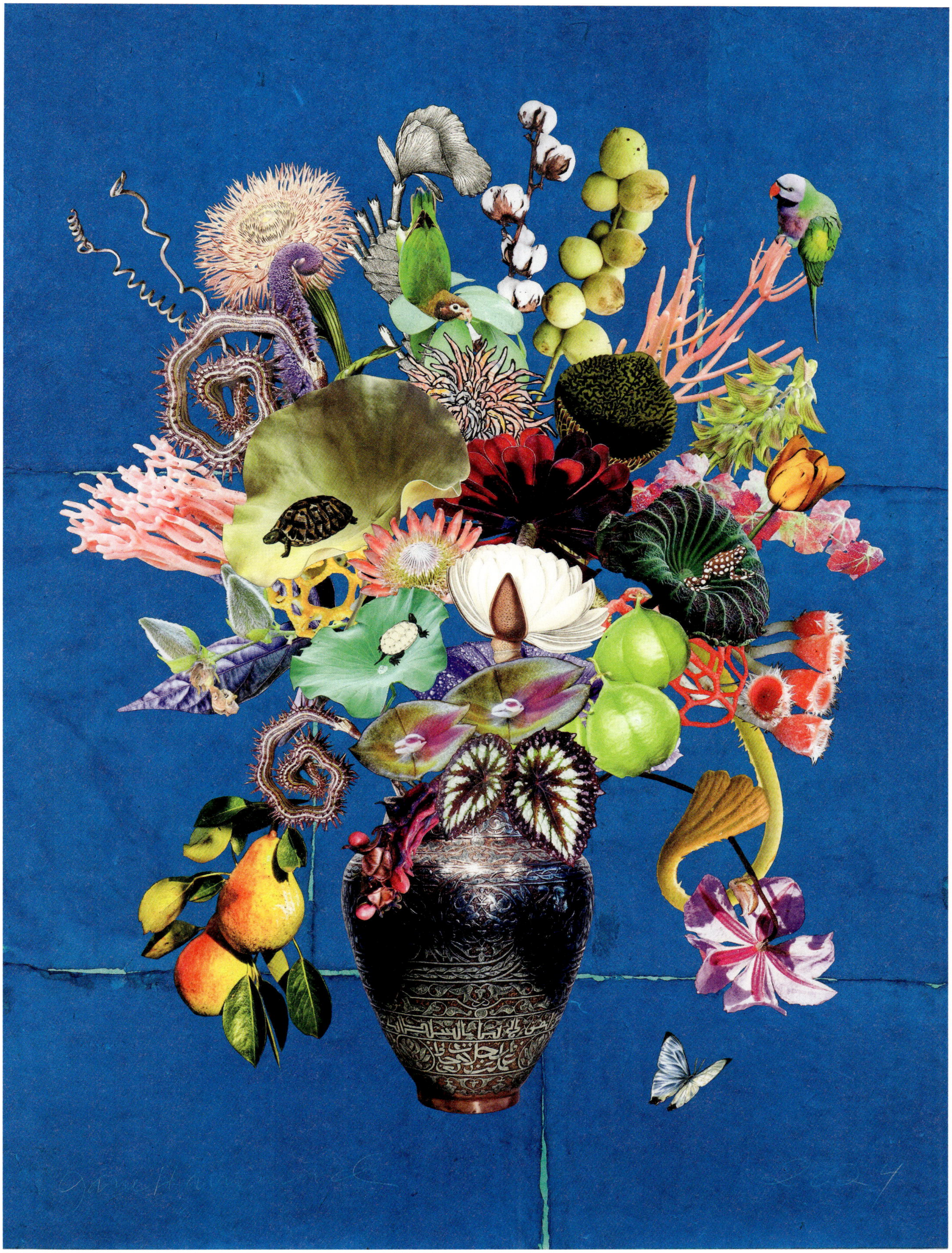

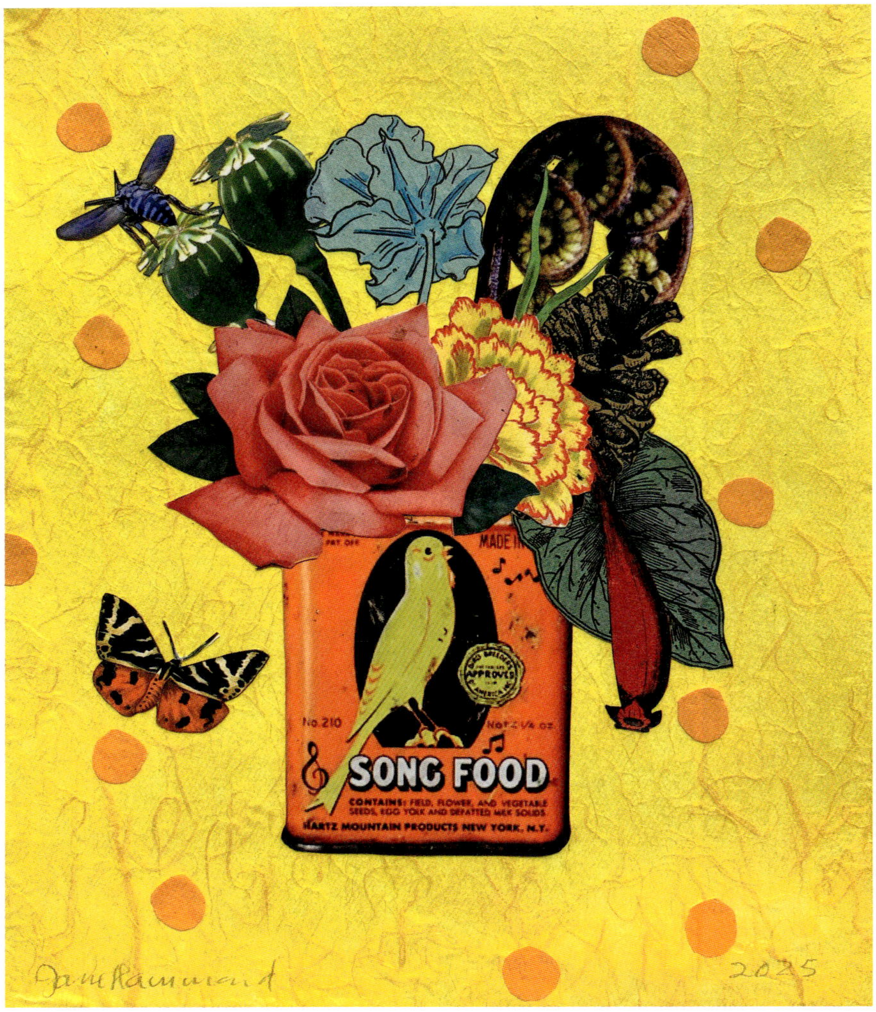

Canary Seed Tin with Tree Fern, Rose and Blue-Banded Bee, 2025
Unique botanical collage using relief printing, digital printing, coloured pencil, Sumi ink, watercolour and gouache, hand cut and assembled on collaged Japanese papers over cotton rag
29.8 × 25.4 cm
11¾ × 10 in

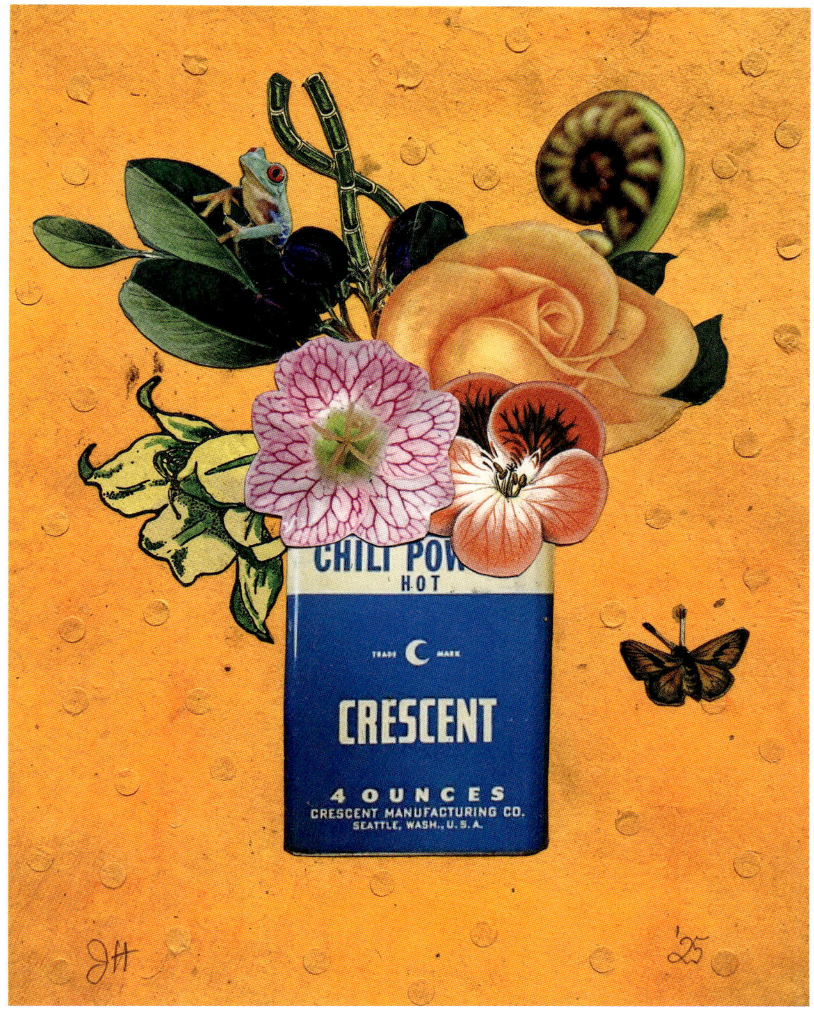

Chili Tin with Tree Fern, Rose and Algae, 2025
Unique botanical collage using relief printing, digital printing, coloured pencil, Sumi ink, watercolour and gouache, hand cut and assembled on collaged Nepali papers over cotton rag
24.8 × 20.3 cm
9¾ × 8 in

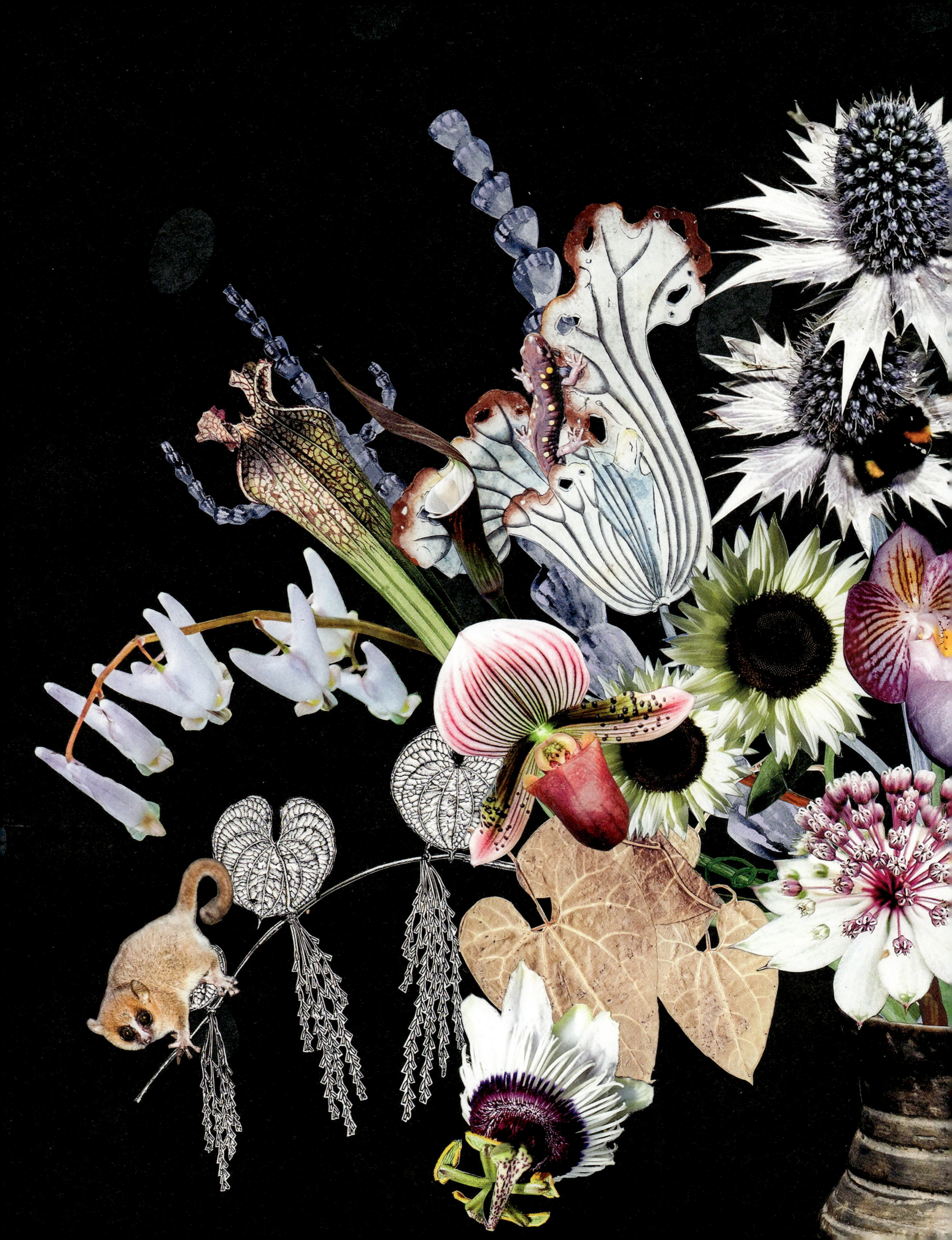

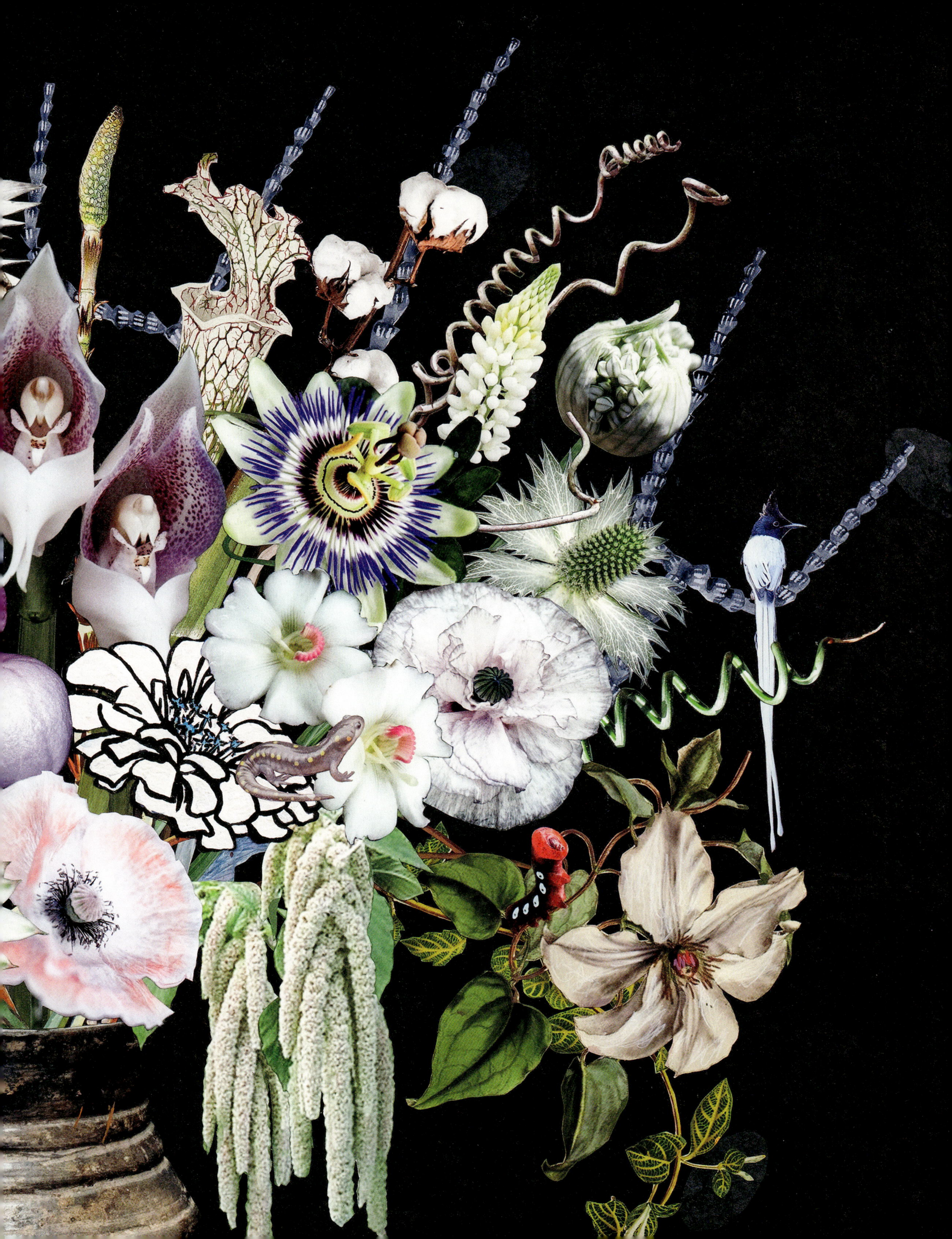

Shang Dynasty Vase with Swaddled Babies, Dutchman's Breeches and Madagascar Mouse Lemur, 2024
Unique botanical collage with relief print, digital printing, coloured pencil, Sumi ink, watercolour and gouache, hand cut and assembled on collaged Nepali paper over cotton rag
96.5 × 127 cm
38 × 50 in

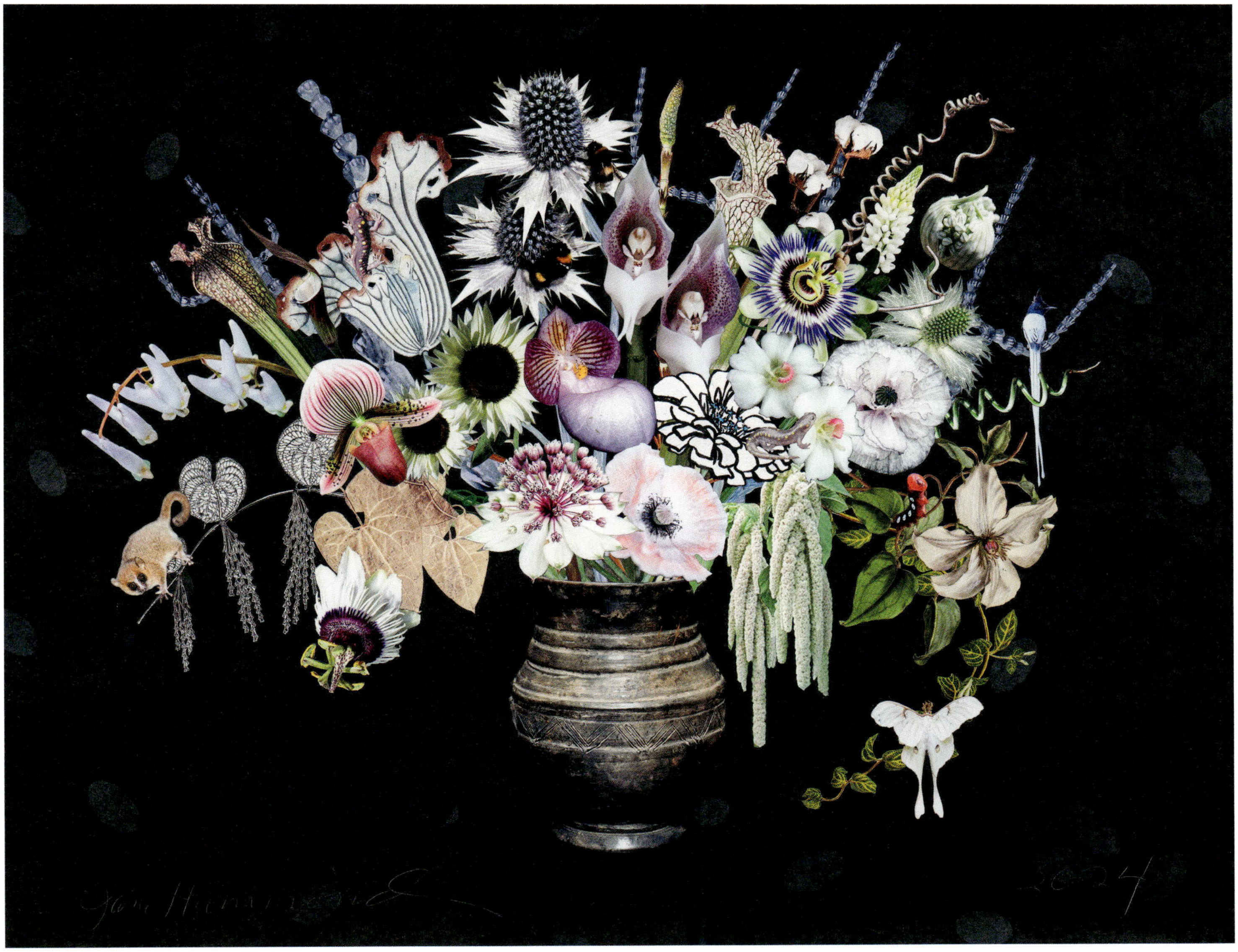

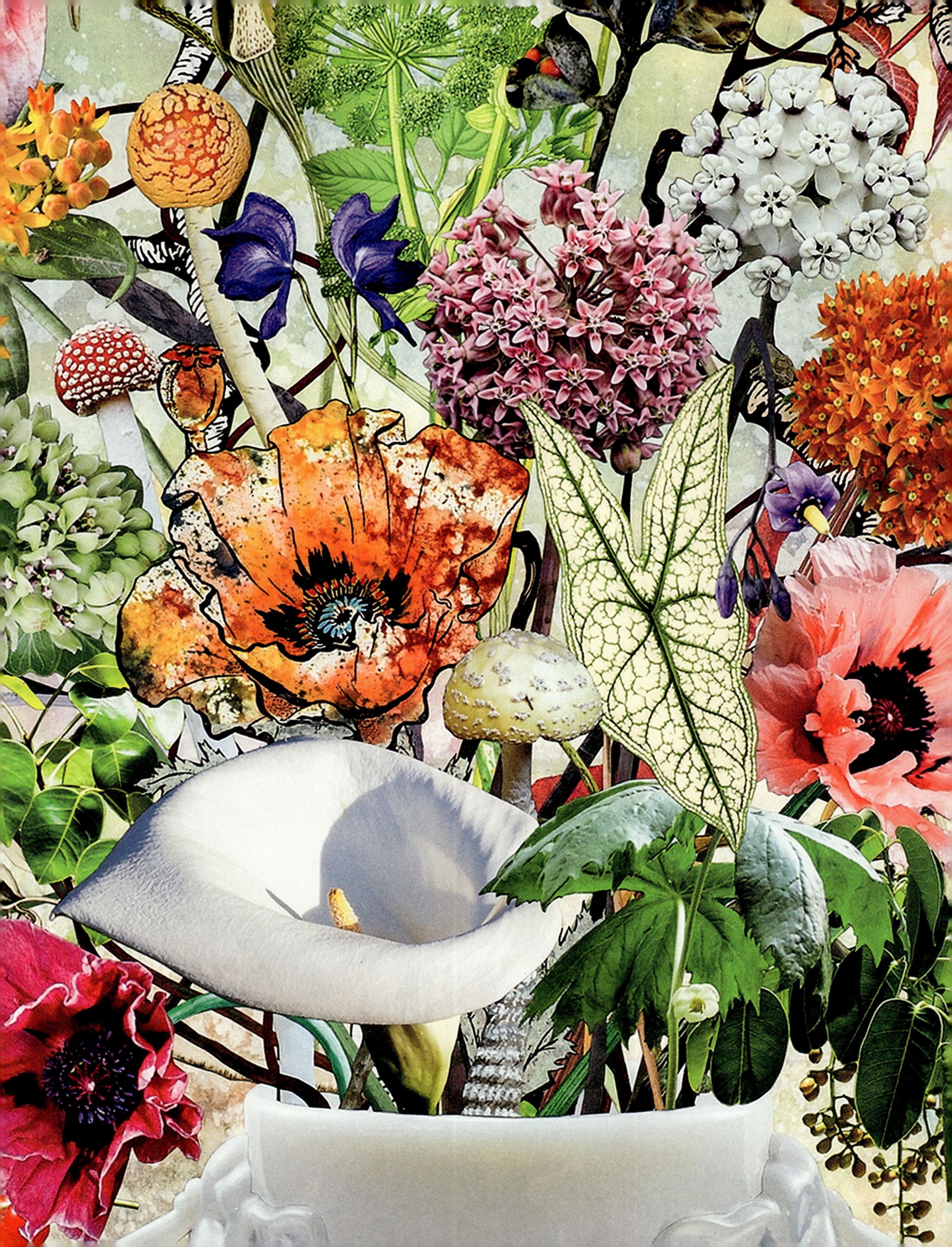

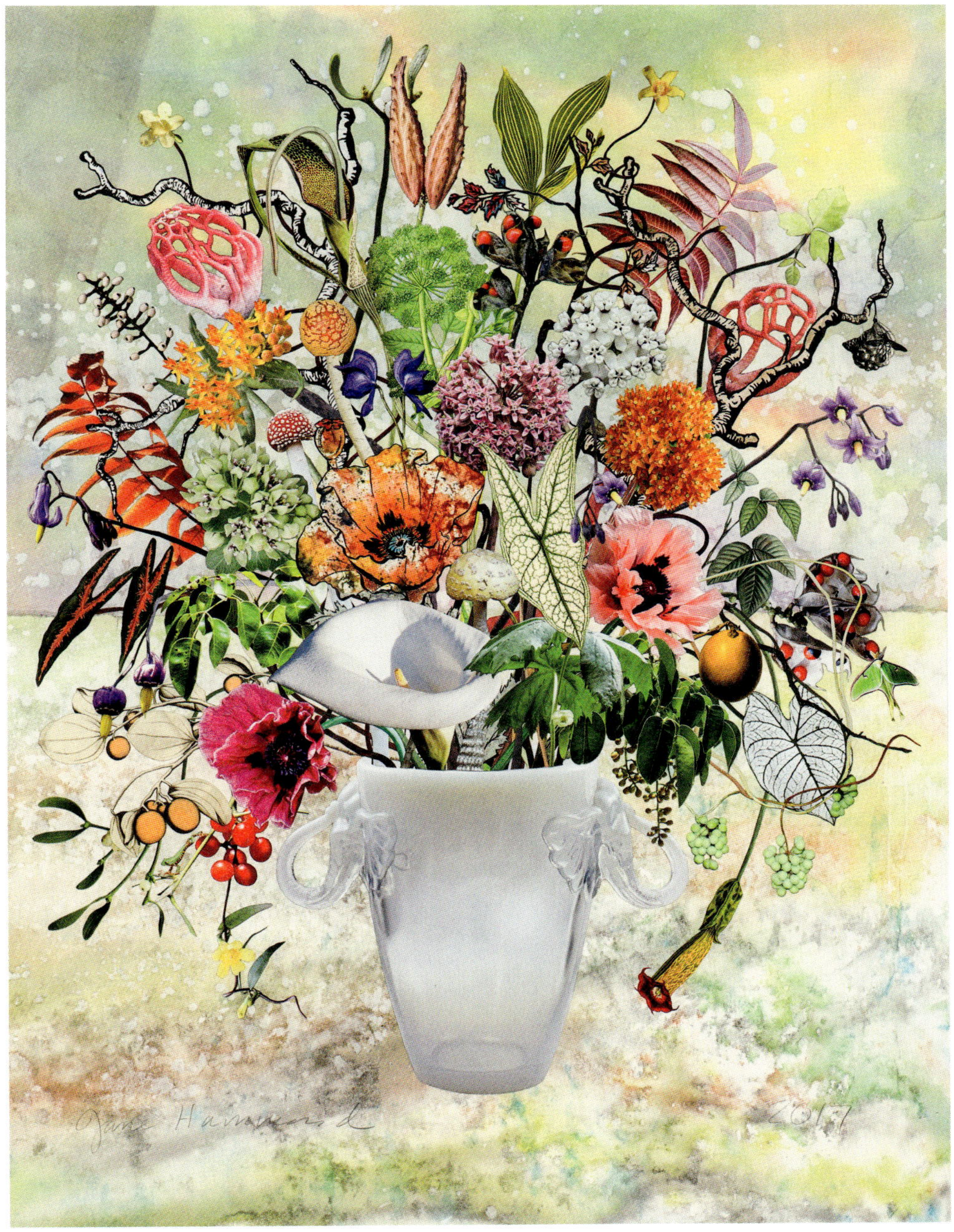

***Elephant Vase with Basket Stinkhorn, Heartbreak Grass and Strychnine*, 2017**
Unique botanical collage using lithography, linocut, relief printing, digital printing, coloured pencil, Sumi ink, watercolour and gouache, hand cut and assembled on collaged hand-painted Japanese papers over cotton rag
127 × 96.5 cm
50 × 38 in

Persian Kashan Vase with Button Medick, Agapanthus and Carmine Bee-Eater, 2024
Unique botanical collage using relief printing, digital printing, coloured pencil, Sumi ink, watercolour and gouache, hand cut and assembled on collaged Japanese papers over cotton rag
127 × 96.5 cm
50 × 38 in

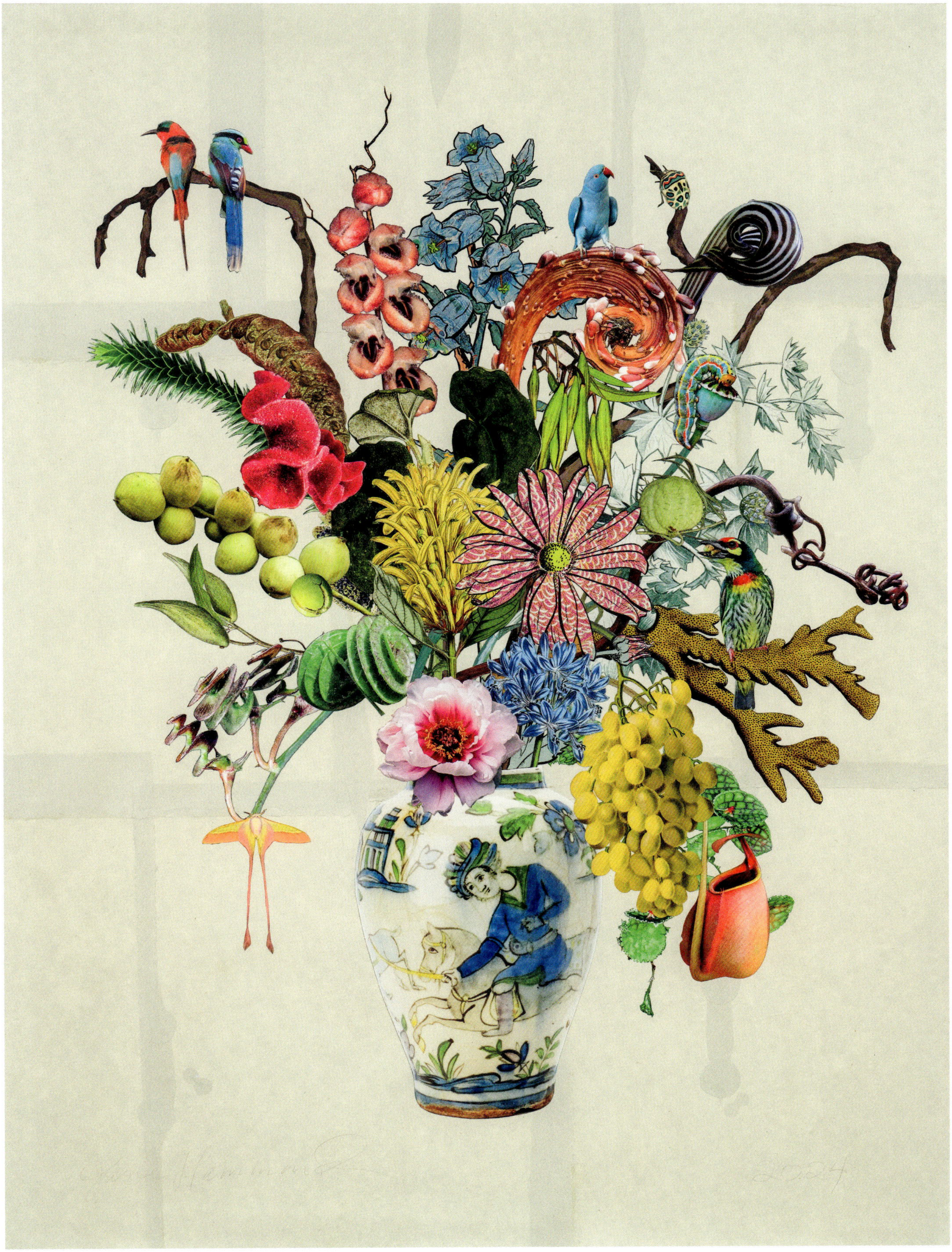

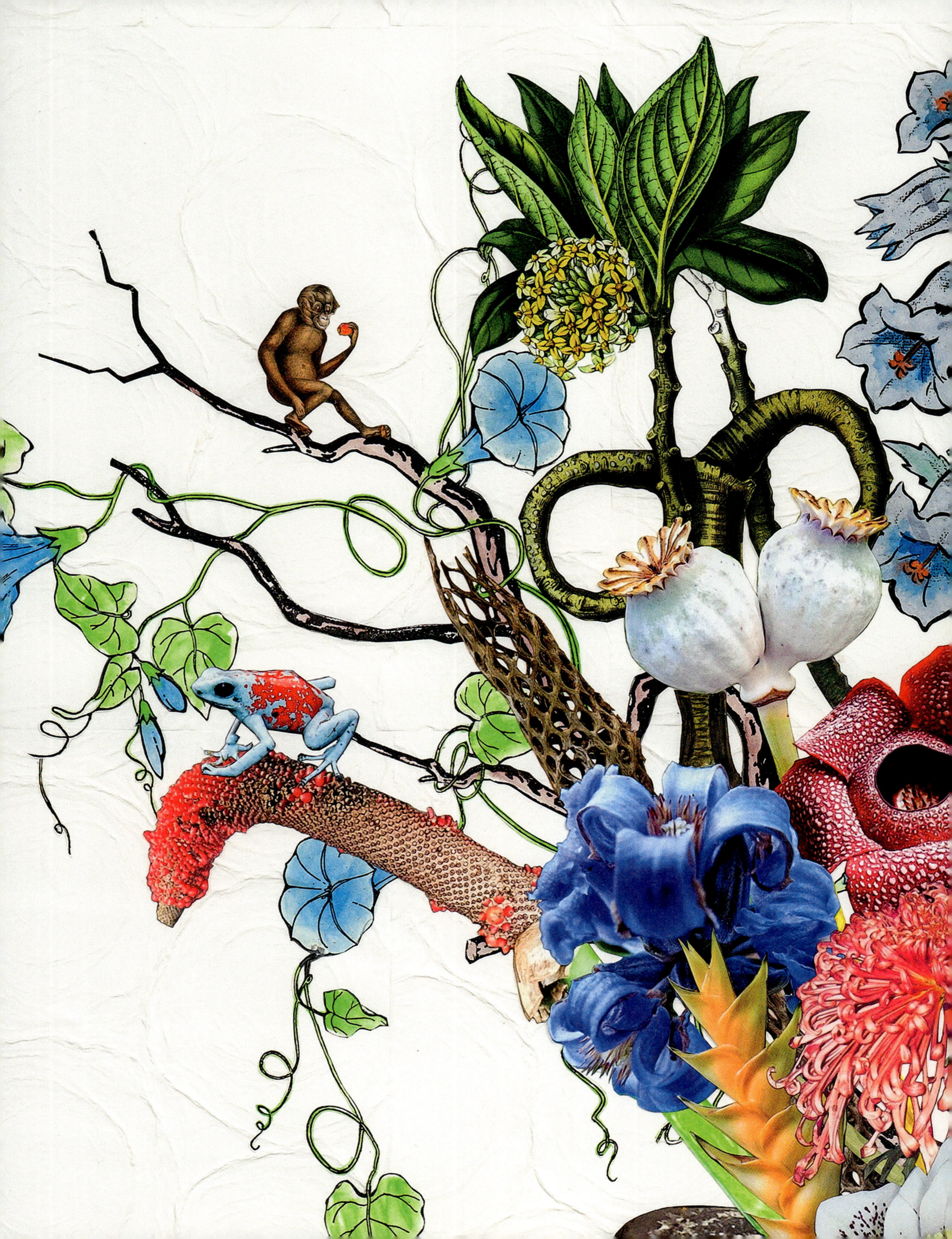

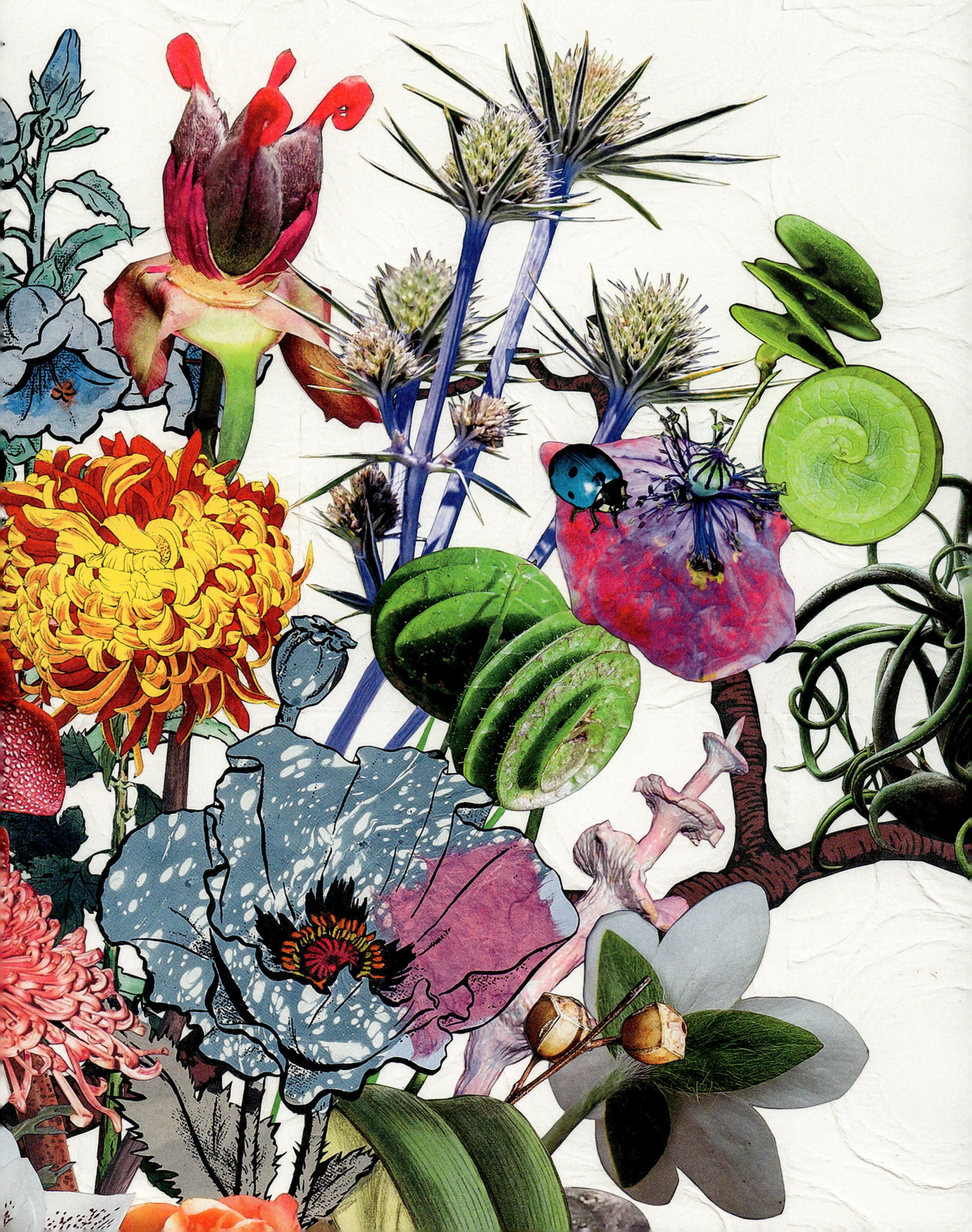

Top Hat Champagne Bucket with Hot Lips, Rafflesia and Button Medick, 2022
Unique botanical collage using linocut, relief printing, digital printing, coloured pencil, Sumi ink, watercolour and gouache, hand cut and assembled on collaged Thai papers over cotton rag
96.5 × 127 cm
38 × 50 in

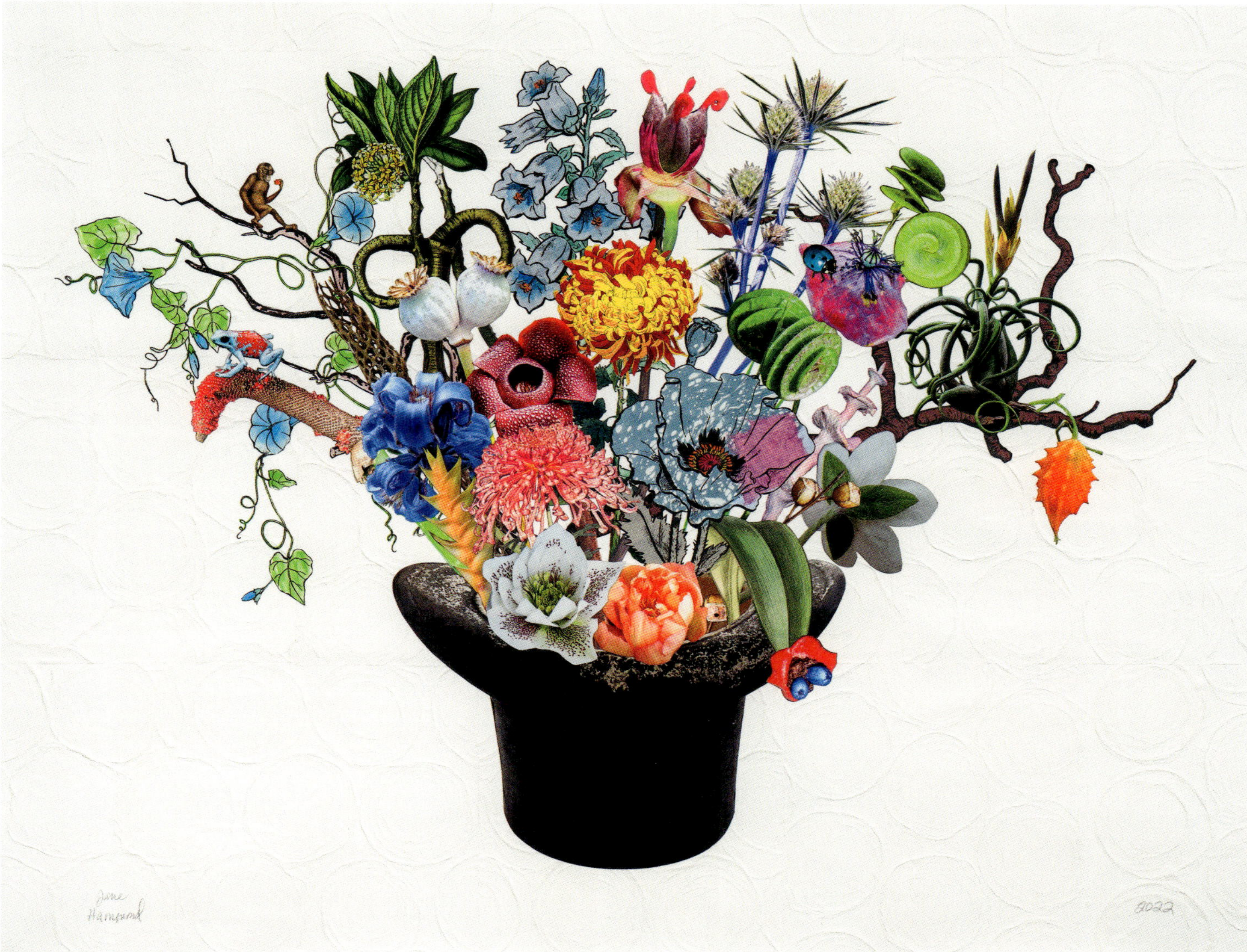

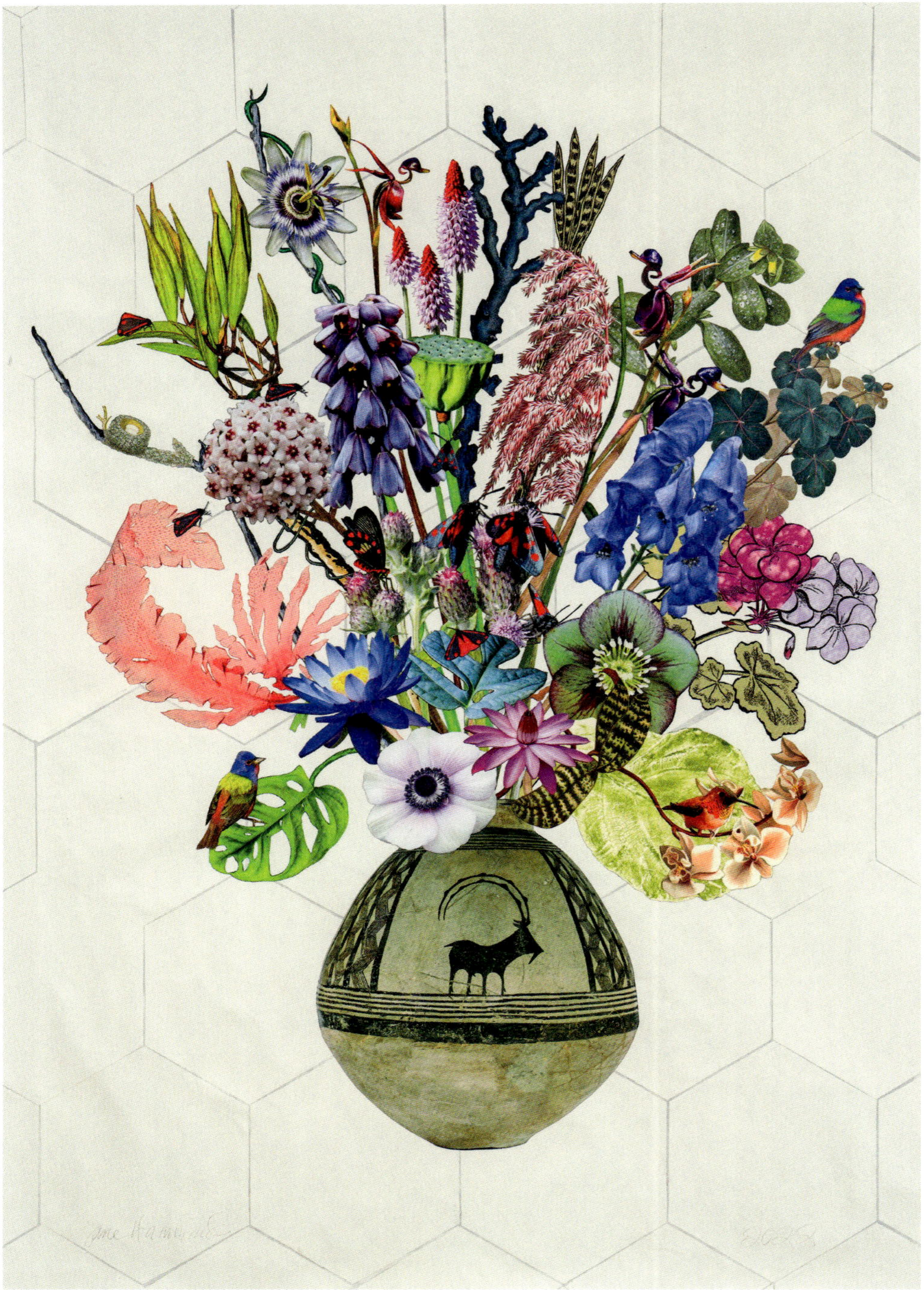

Persian Goat Vase with Lotus, Monkshood and Passion Flower, 2022
Unique botanical collage using relief printing, collagraph, digital printing, coloured pencil, Sumi ink, watercolour and gouache, hand cut and assembled on collaged clay-coated paper over painted cotton rag
127 × 91.4 cm
50 × 36 in

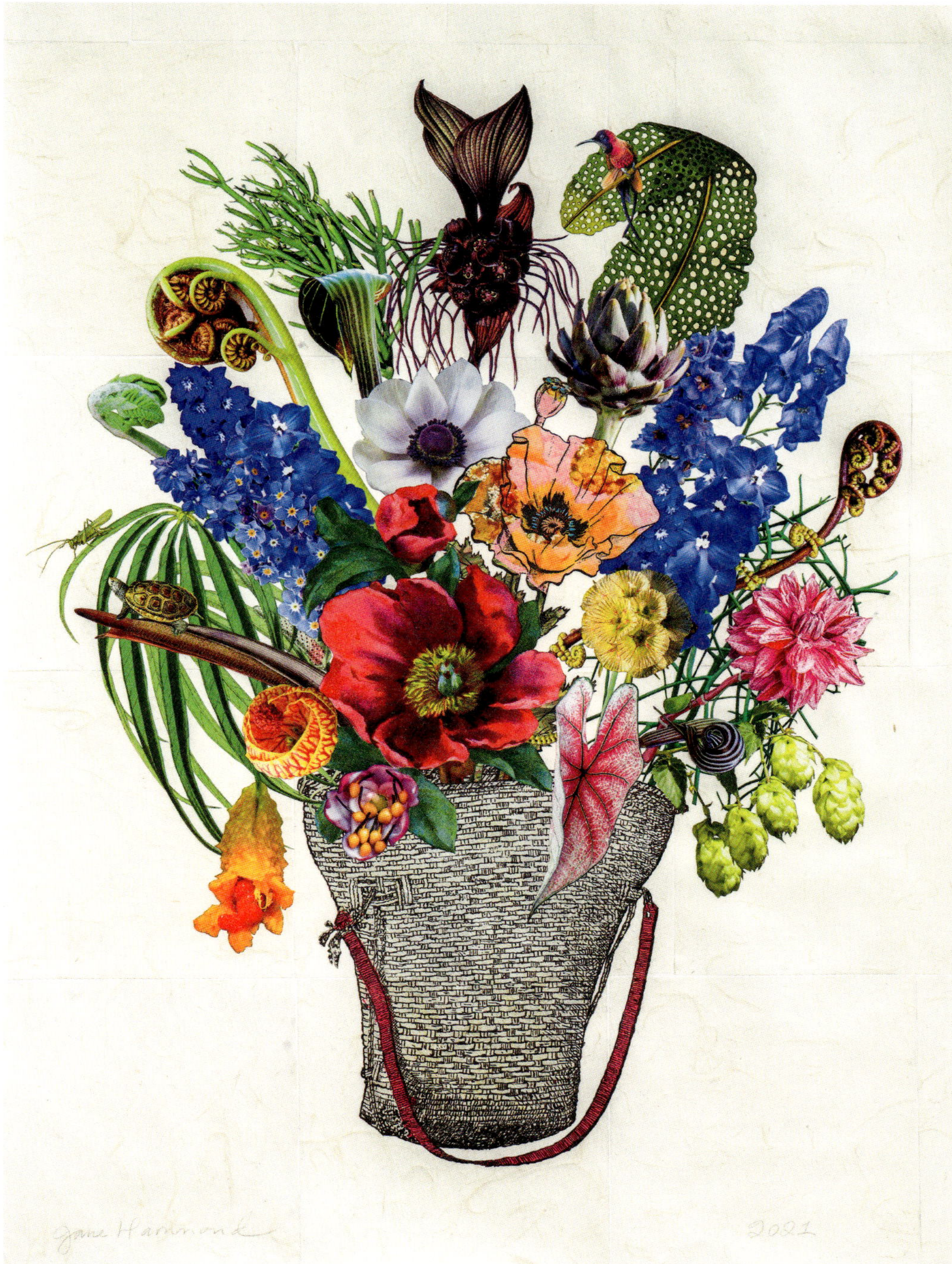

***Choctaw Carrying Basket with Bat Lily, Axinaea and Green Cone-Headed Plant Hopper*, 2021**
Unique botanical collage using relief printing, digital printing, coloured pencil, Sumi ink, watercolour, gouache and two kinds of silver leaf, hand cut and assembled on collaged Japanese papers over cotton rag
127 × 96.5 cm
50 × 38 in

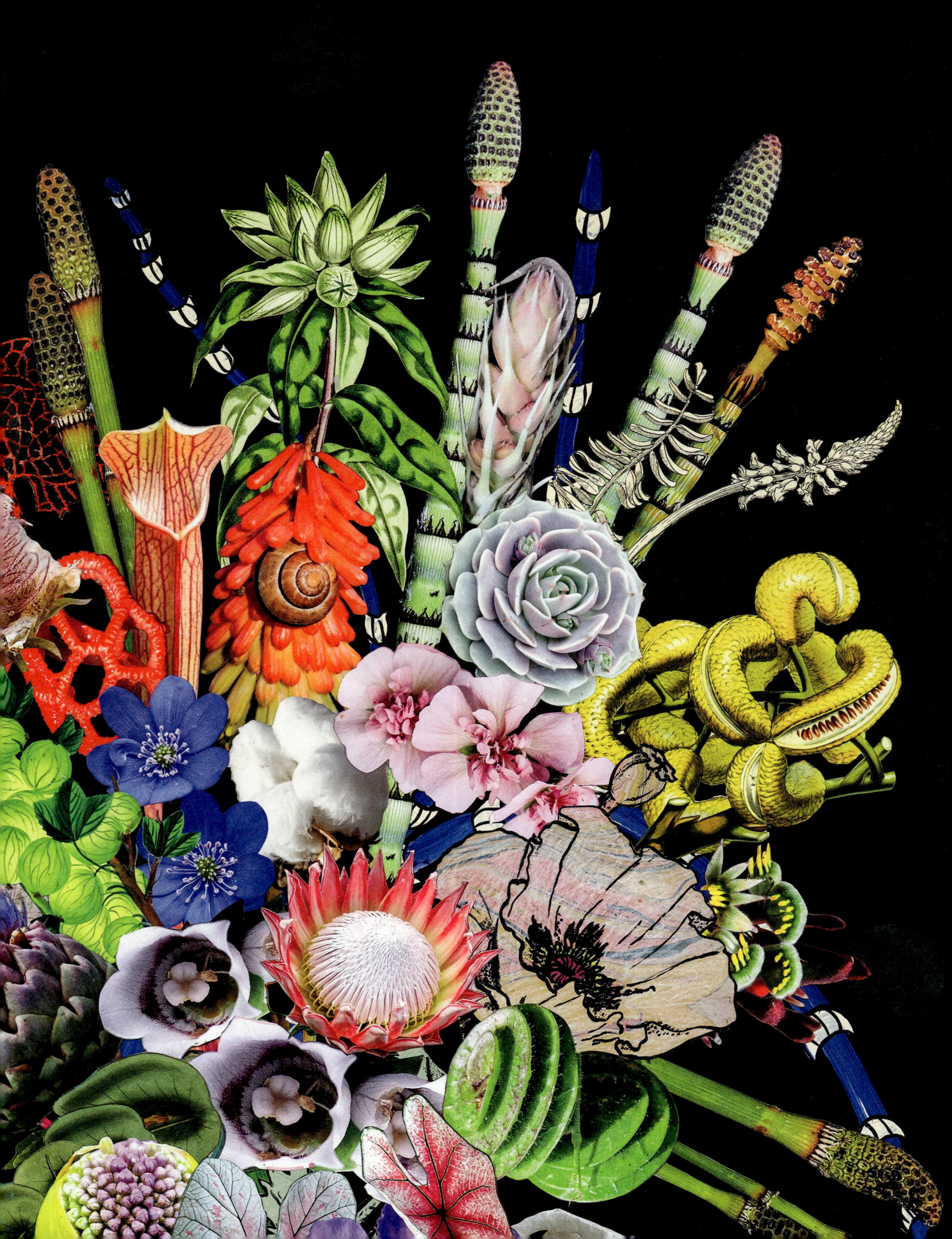

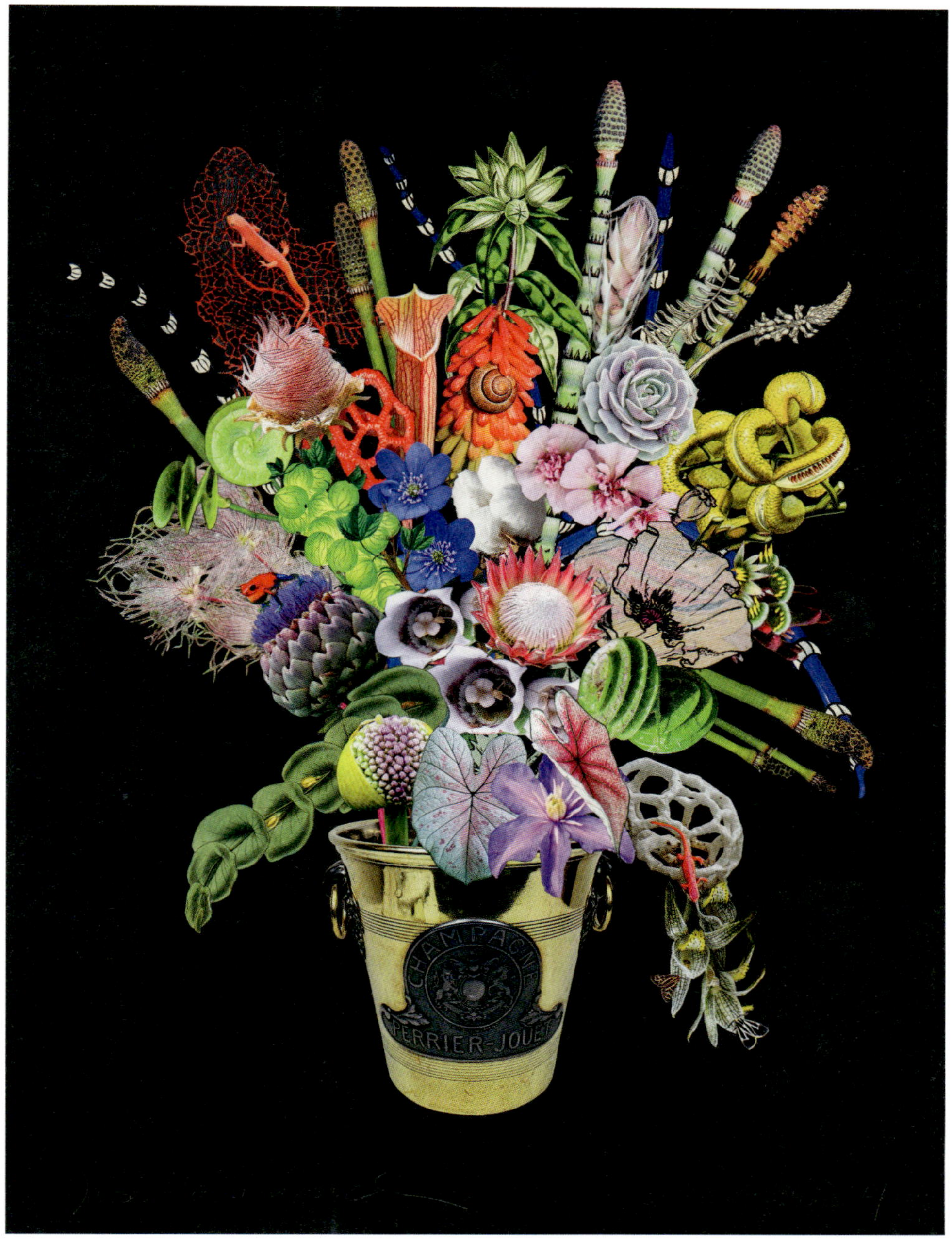

Champagne Bucket with Prairie Smoke, Gooseberries and Two Red Efts, 2024
Unique botanical collage using relief printing, digital printing, coloured pencil, Sumi ink, watercolour and gouache, hand cut and assembled on collaged Nepali papers over cotton rag
127 × 96.5 cm
50 × 38 in

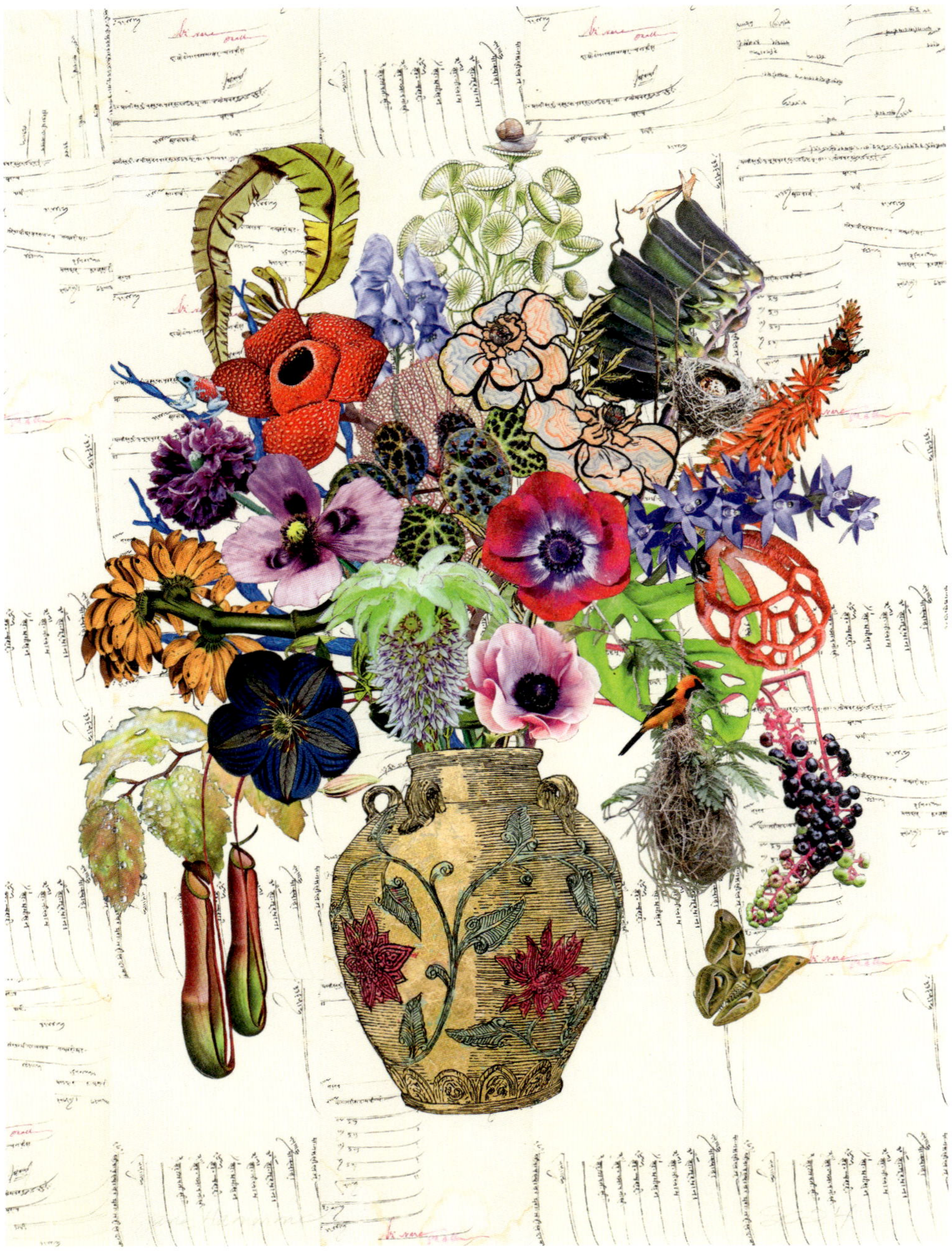

Korean Vase with Baltimore Oriole and Nest, Scented Sun Orchid and Pineapple Lily, 2024
Unique botanical collage with relief print, digital printing, coloured pencil, Sumi ink, watercolour, gouache, gold leaf and dyed silver leaf, hand cut and assembled on collaged digital prints of Indian ledger papers over cotton rag
127 × 96.5 cm
50 × 38 in

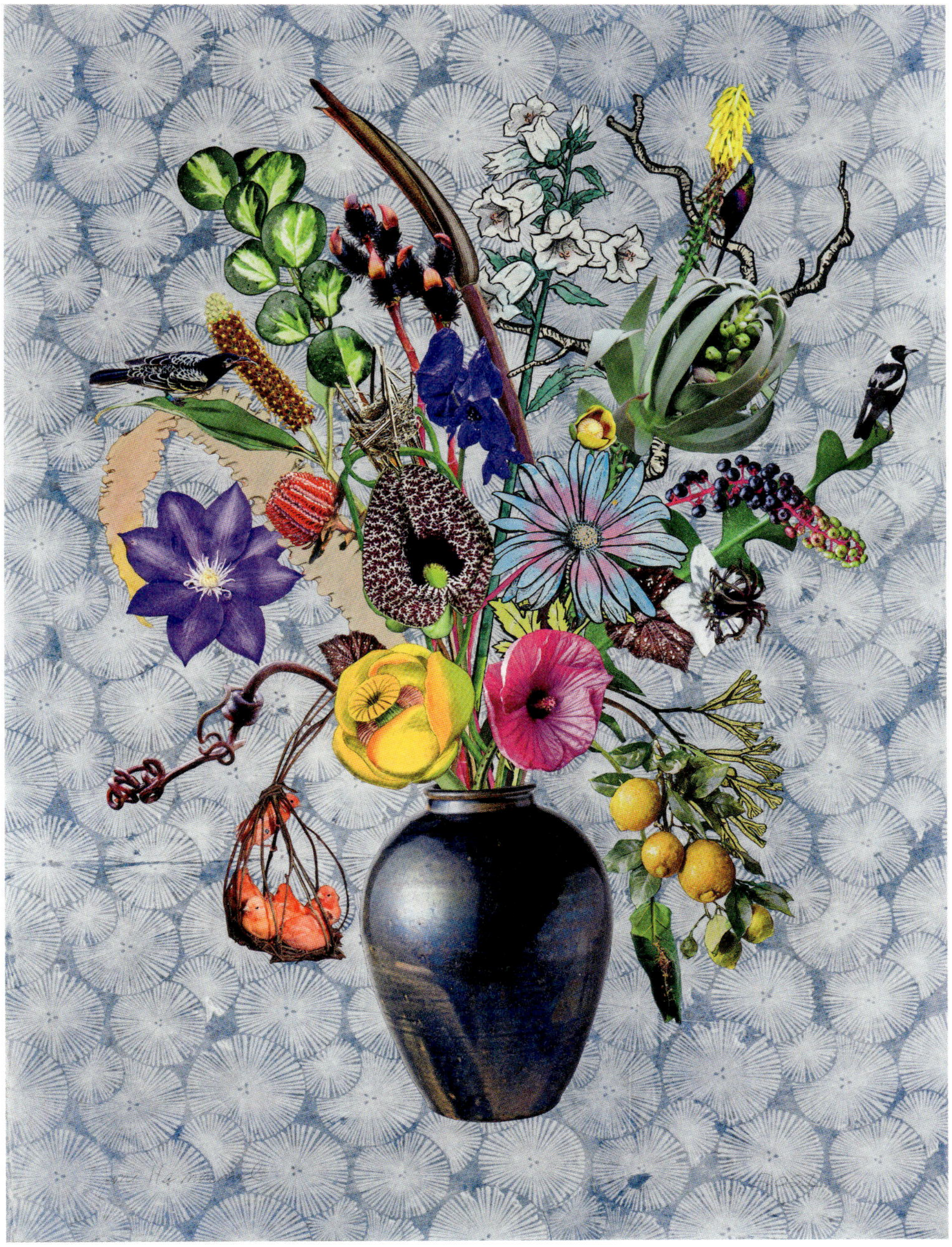

Japanese Vase with Canterbury Bells, Clematis H.F. Young and Red-Factor Canaries, 2021
Unique botanical collage using linocut, relief printing, digital printing, coloured pencil, Sumi ink, watercolour and gouache, hand cut and assembled on collaged Japanese papers over painted cotton rag
127 × 96.5 cm
50 × 38 in

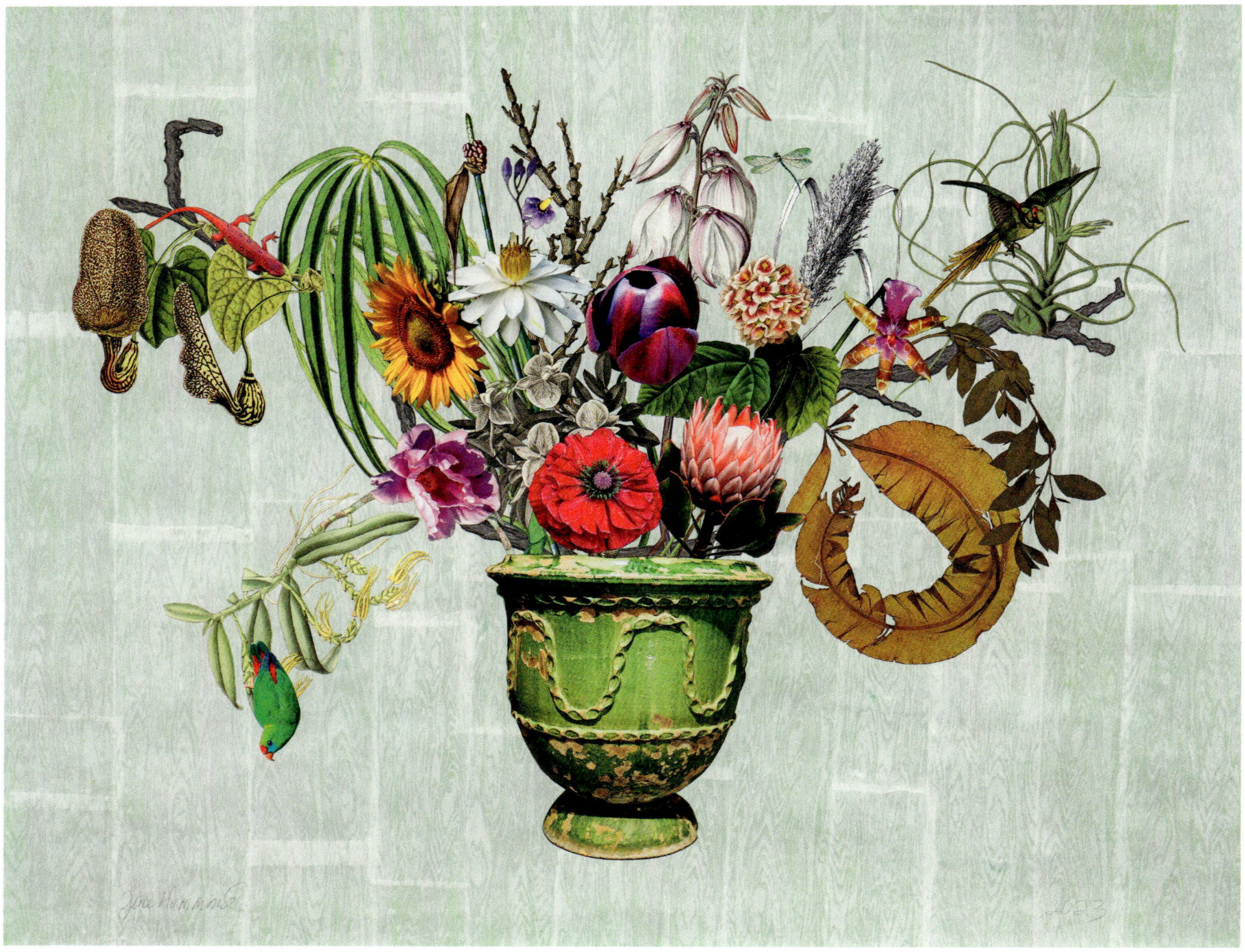

French Garden Urn with Spanish Dagger, Dutchman's Pipe and Malaysian Hanging Parrot, 2023
Unique botanical collage using digital printing, coloured pencil, Sumi ink, watercolour and gouache, hand cut and assembled on collaged Japanese papers over painted cotton rag
96.5 × 127 cm
38 × 50 in

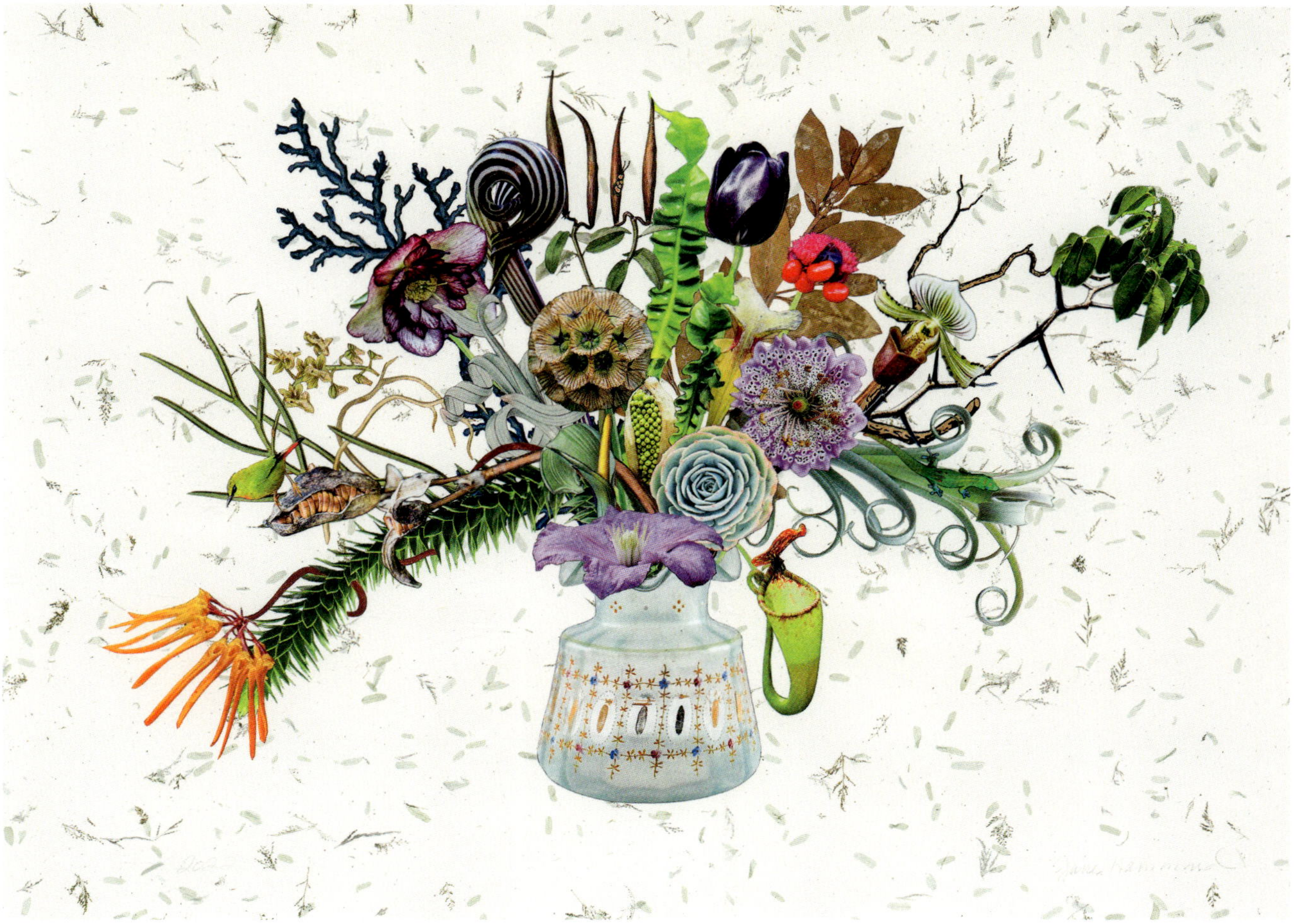

Venetian Glass with Hellebore, Hearts-a-bustin' and Black Tulip, 2022
Unique botanical collage using linocut, digital printing, coloured pencil, Sumi ink, watercolour and gouache, hand cut and assembled on collaged Japanese papers over cotton rag
71.1 × 98.4 cm
28 × 38¾ in

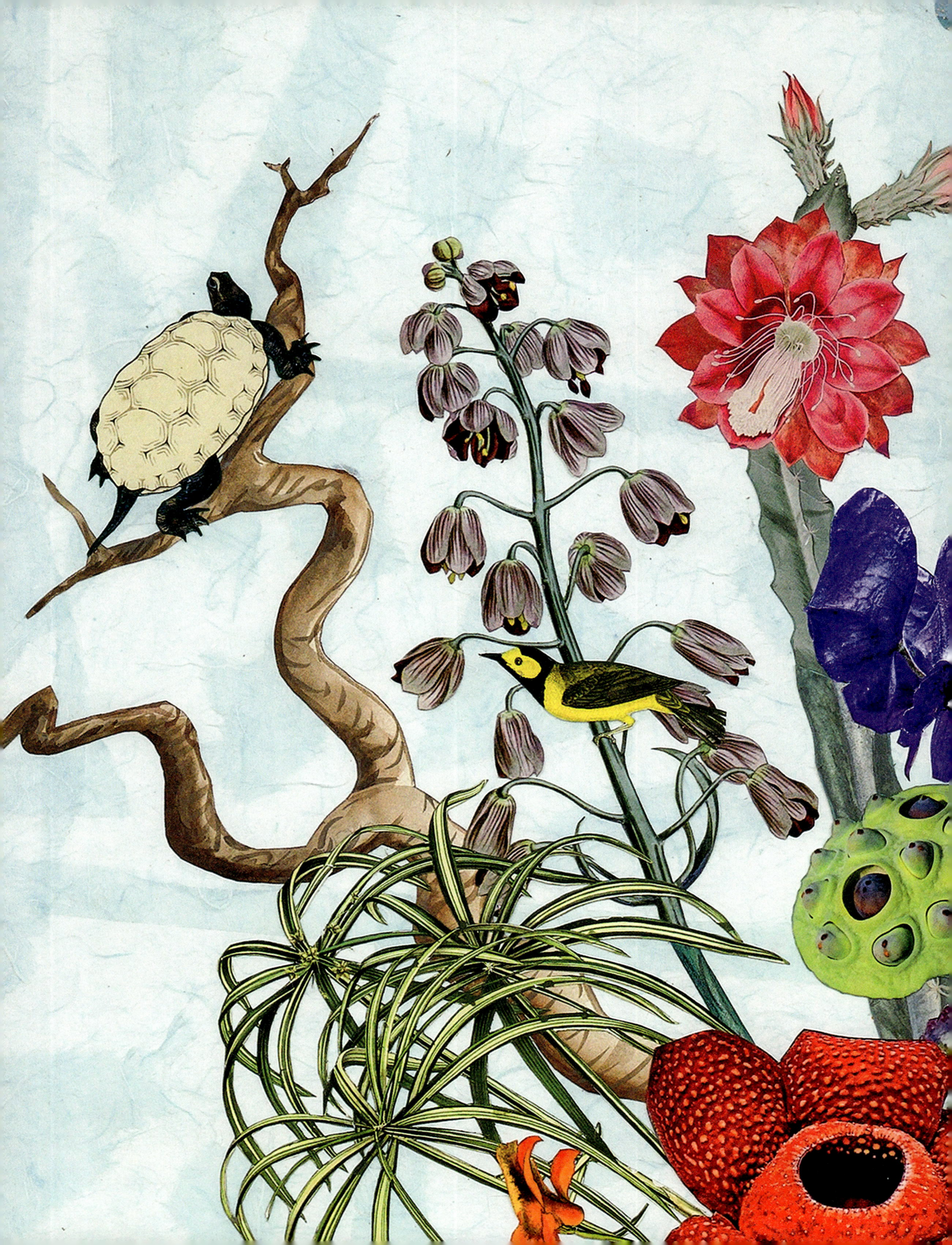

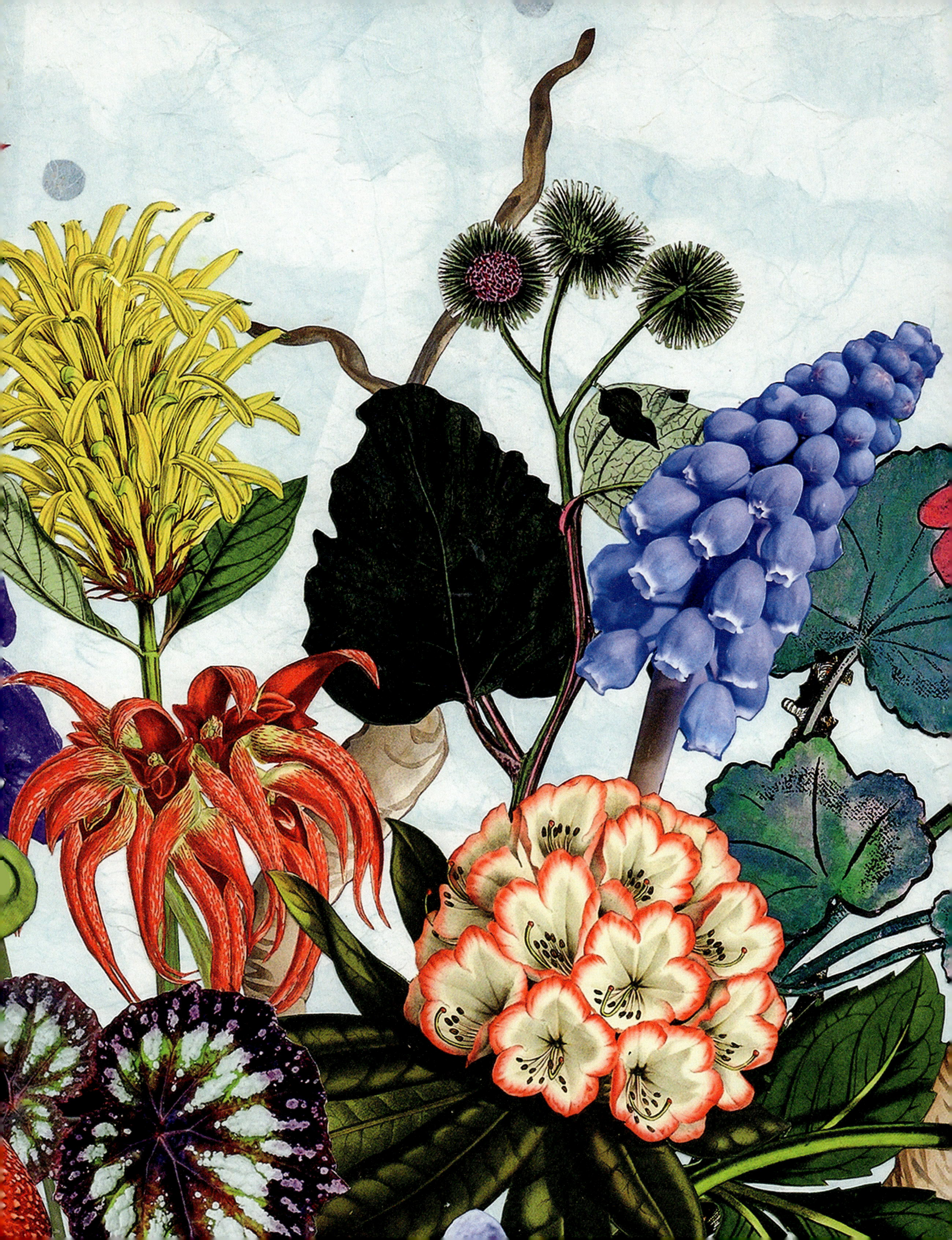

Crown-Shaped Champagne Bucket with Monkshood, Fritillaria Persica and Cecropia Moth, 2023
Unique botanical collage using relief printing, digital printing, coloured pencil, Sumi ink, watercolour and gouache, hand cut and assembled on collaged Japanese papers over cotton rag
96.5 × 127 cm
38 × 50 in

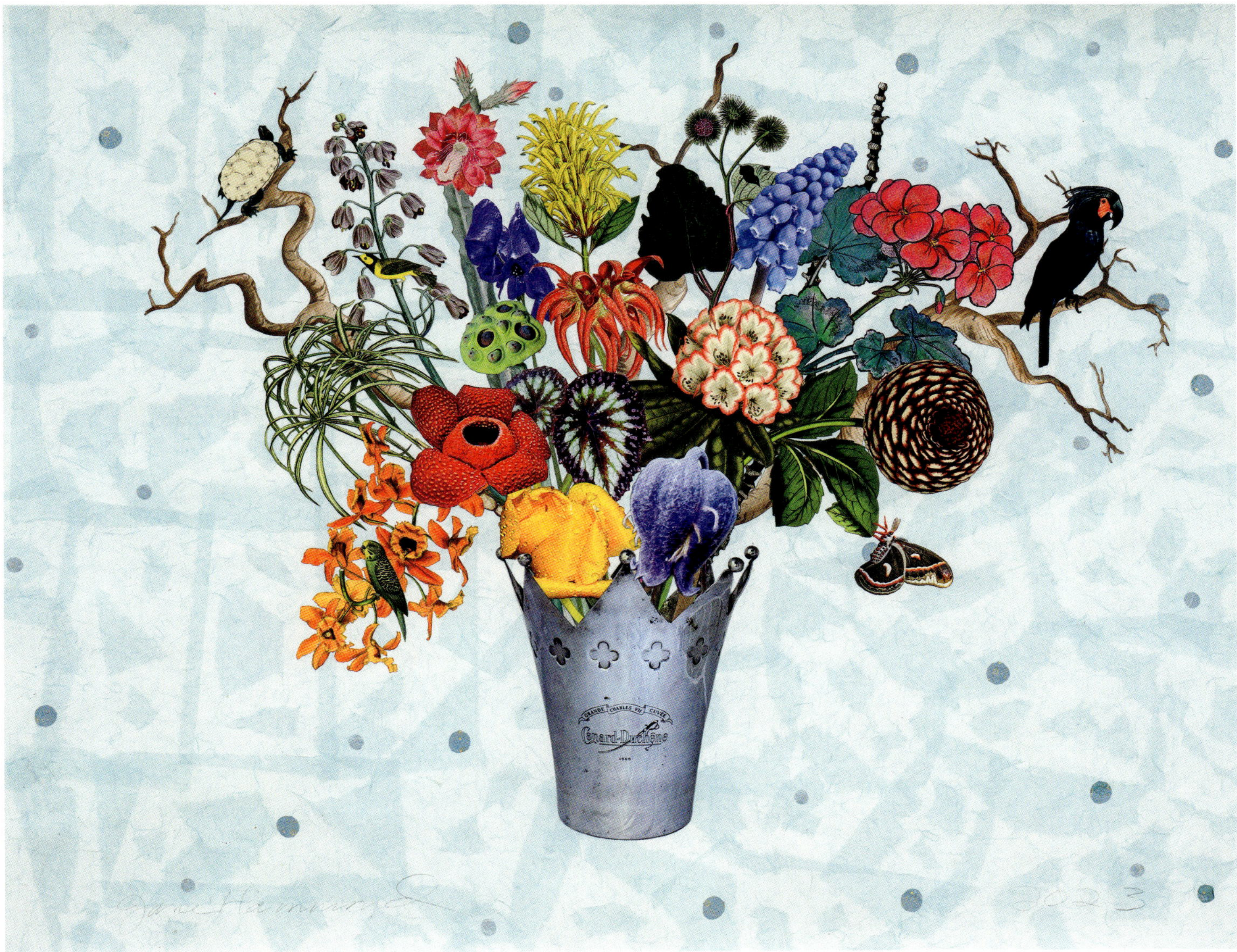

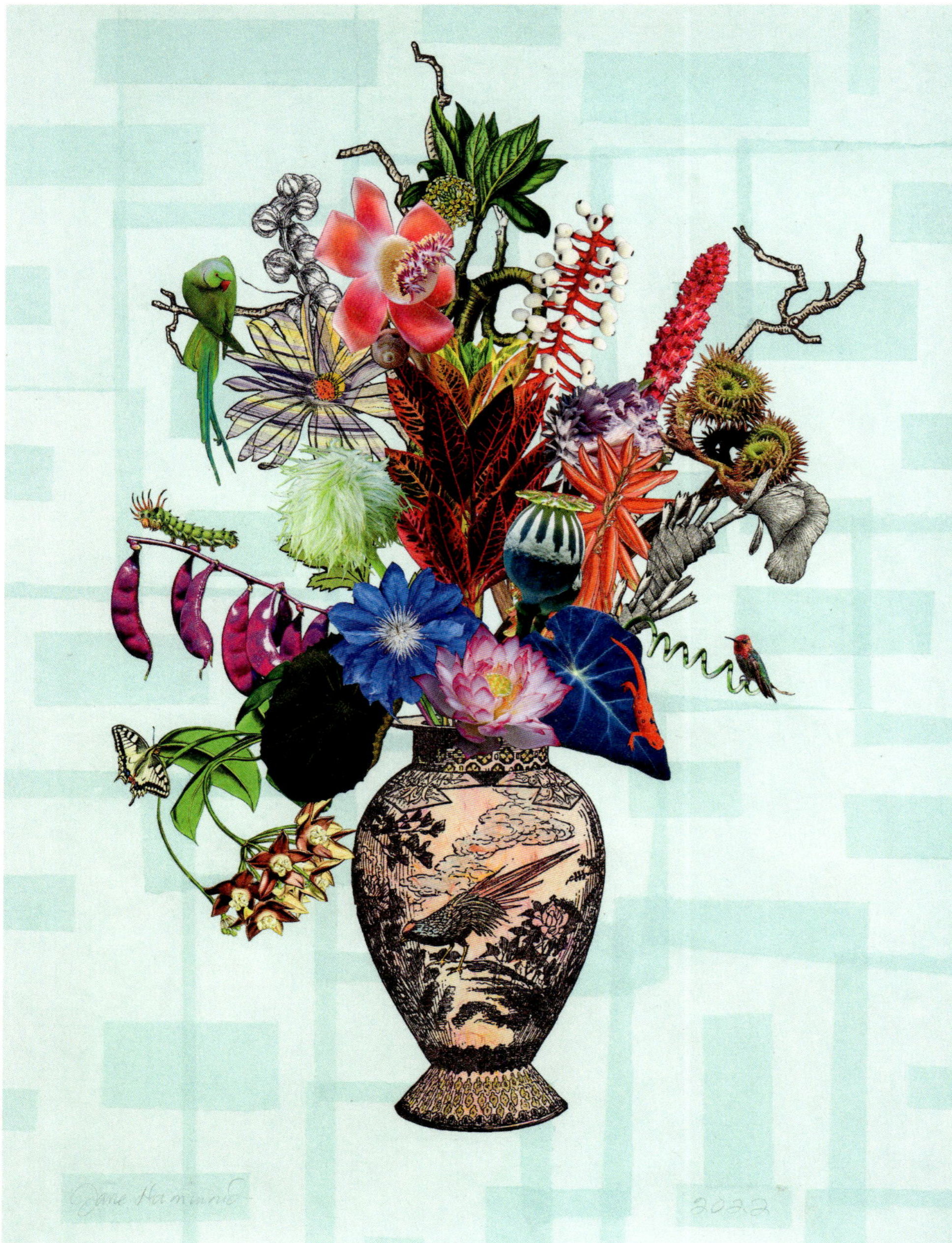

Chinese Bird Vase with Cannonball Tree Flower, Red Eft and Doll's Eyes, 2022
Unique botanical collage using relief printing, digital printing, coloured pencil, Sumi ink, watercolour, gouache and mica, hand cut and assembled on collaged Japanese papers over cotton rag
127 × 96.5 cm
50 × 38 in

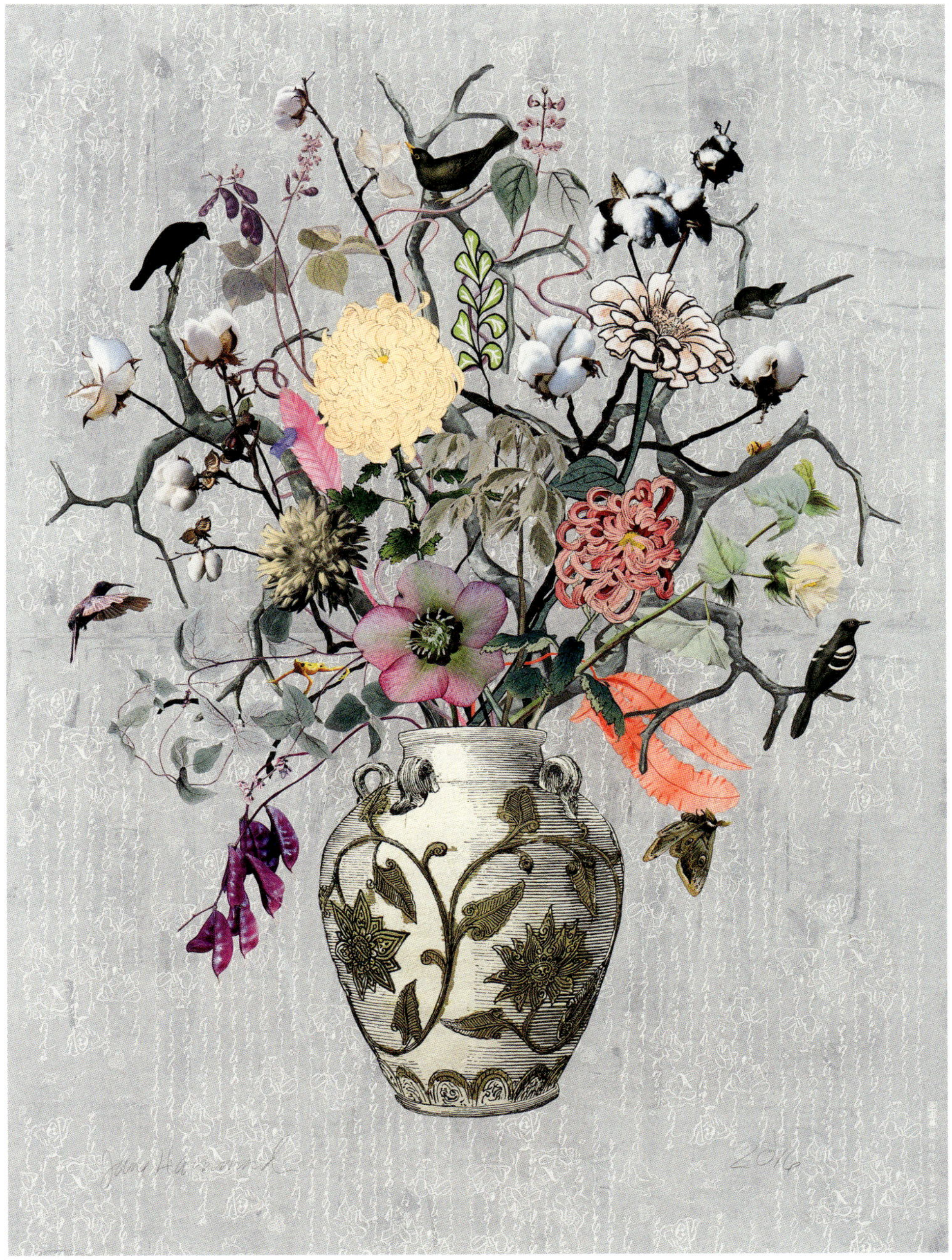

Korean Vase with Hyacinth Beans, Cotton and Chrysanthemum, 2016
Unique botanical collage using lithography, linocut, relief printing, digital printing, coloured pencil, Sumi ink, watercolour, gouache, silver leaf and bronze leaf, hand cut and assembled on collaged Japanese papers over painted cotton rag
127 × 96.5 cm
50 × 38 in

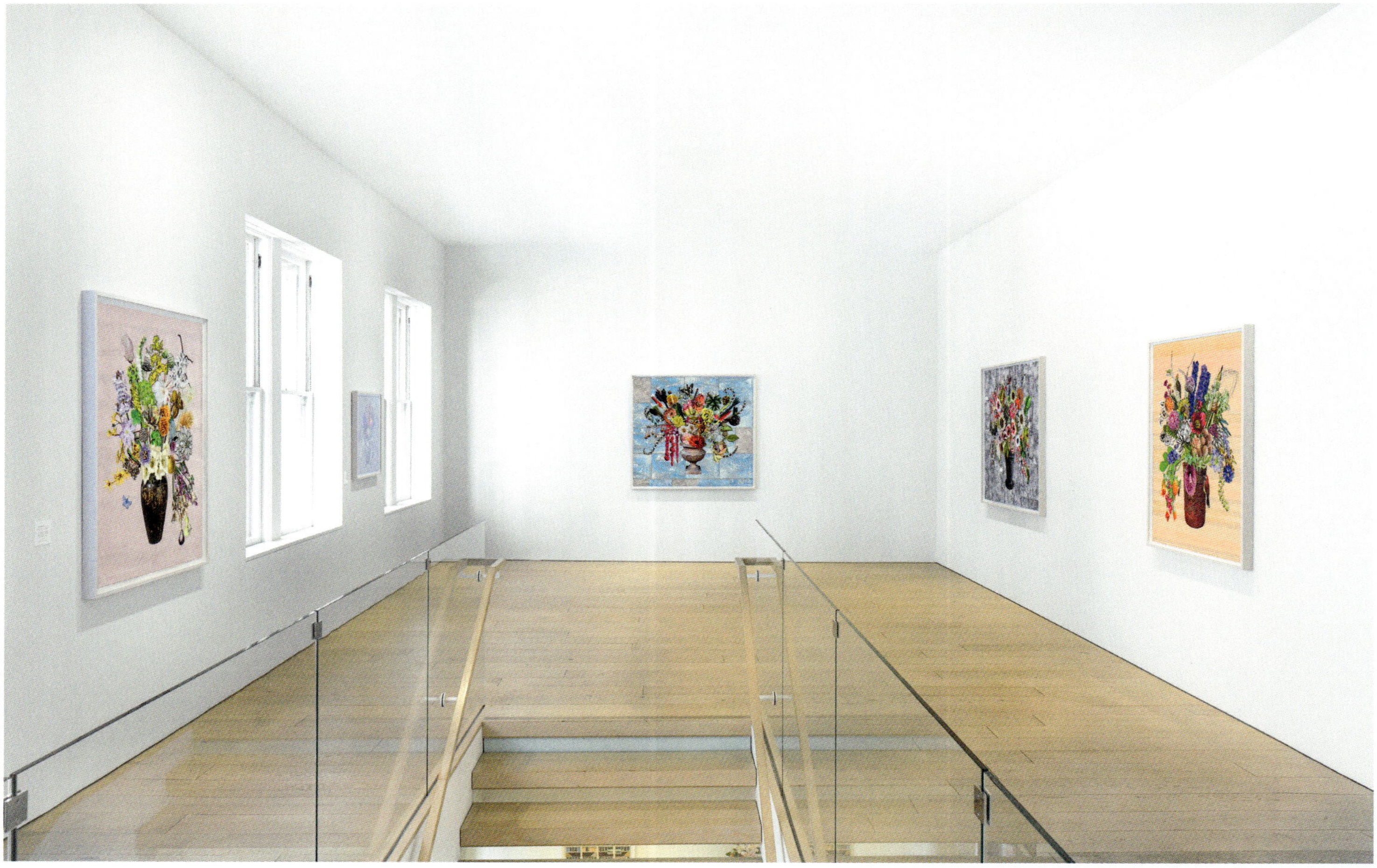

Exhibition views of *Jane Hammond: Chocolate Cosmos, String of Pearls*
Berggruen Gallery, San Francisco
23 October 2025 – 8 January 2026

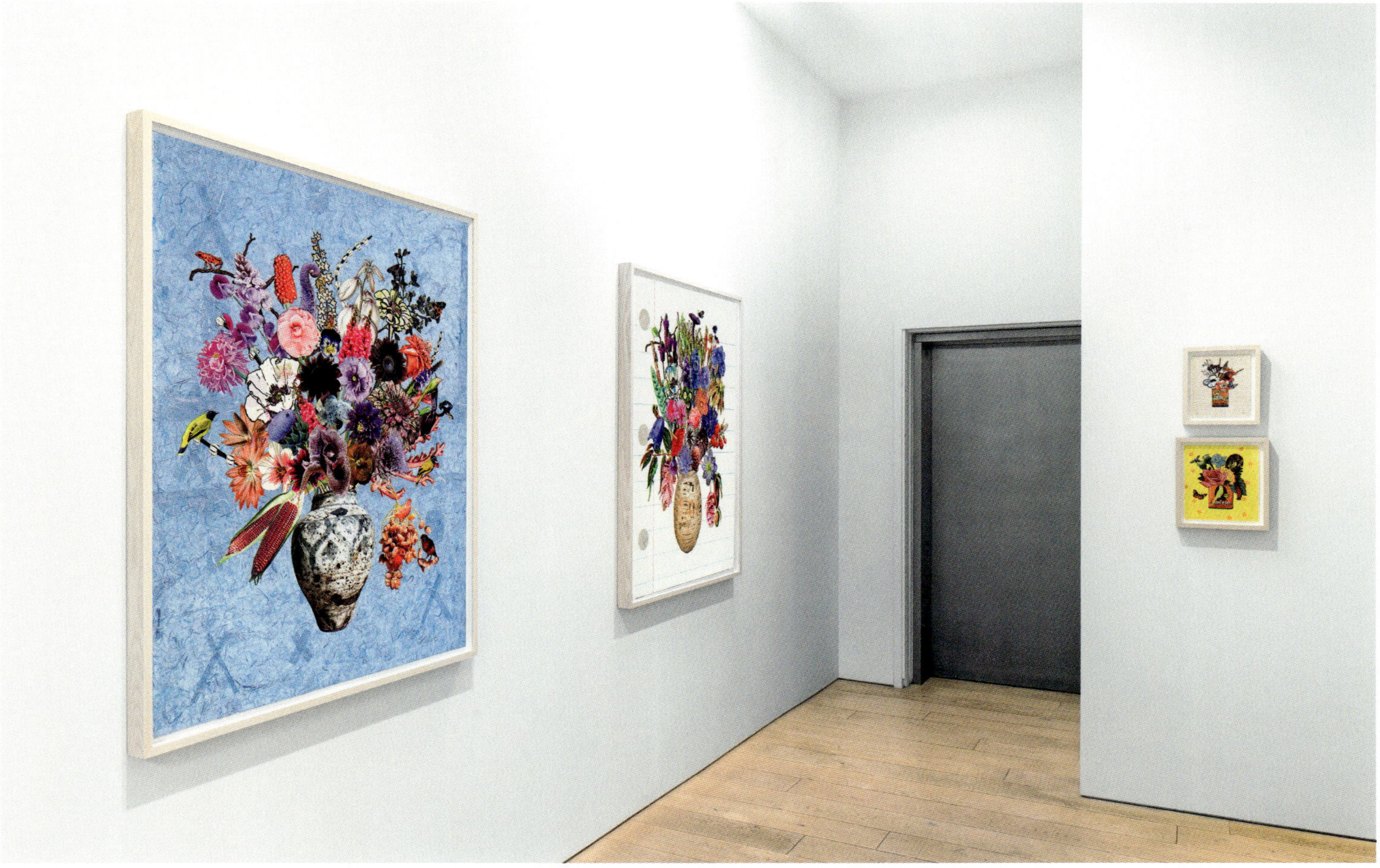

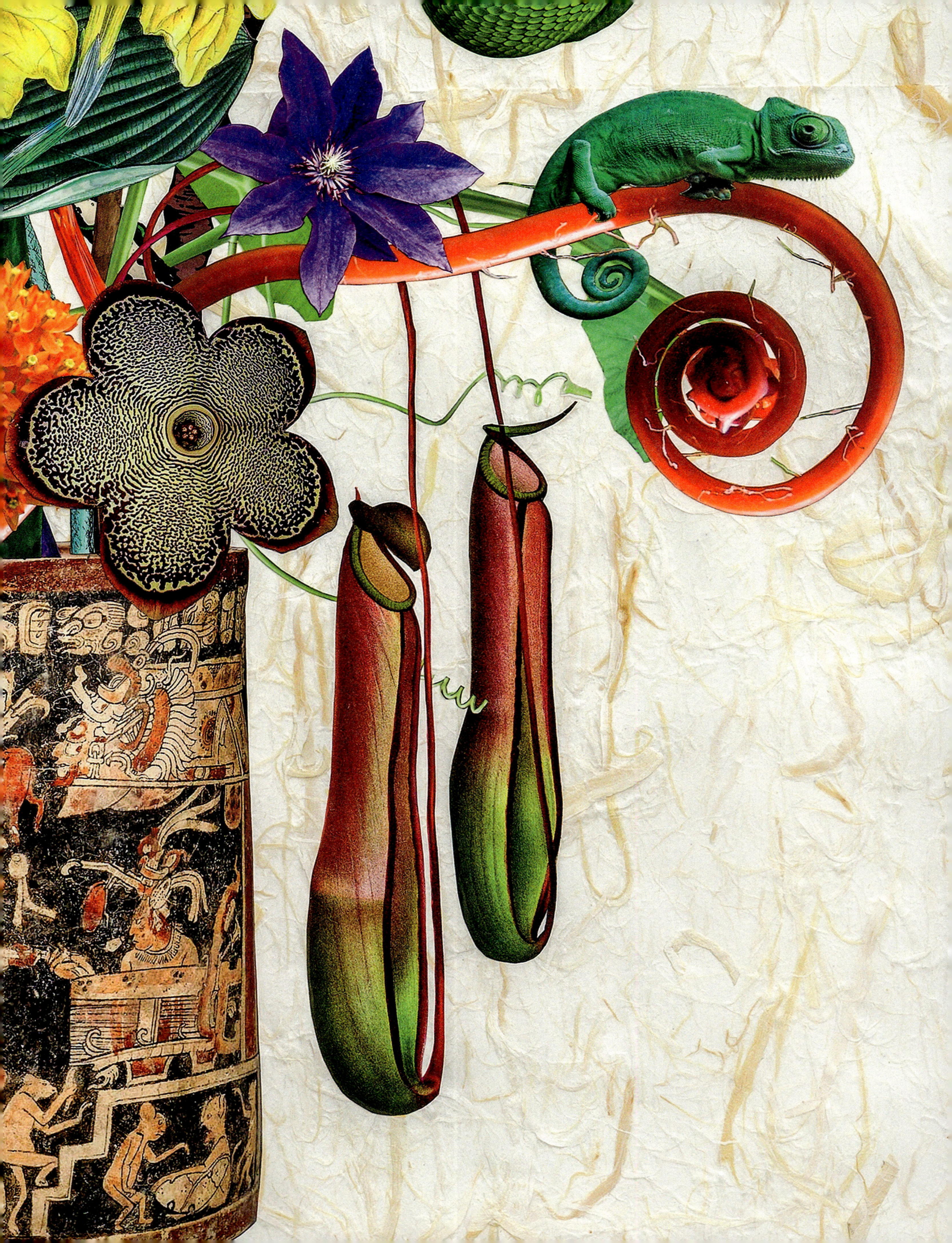

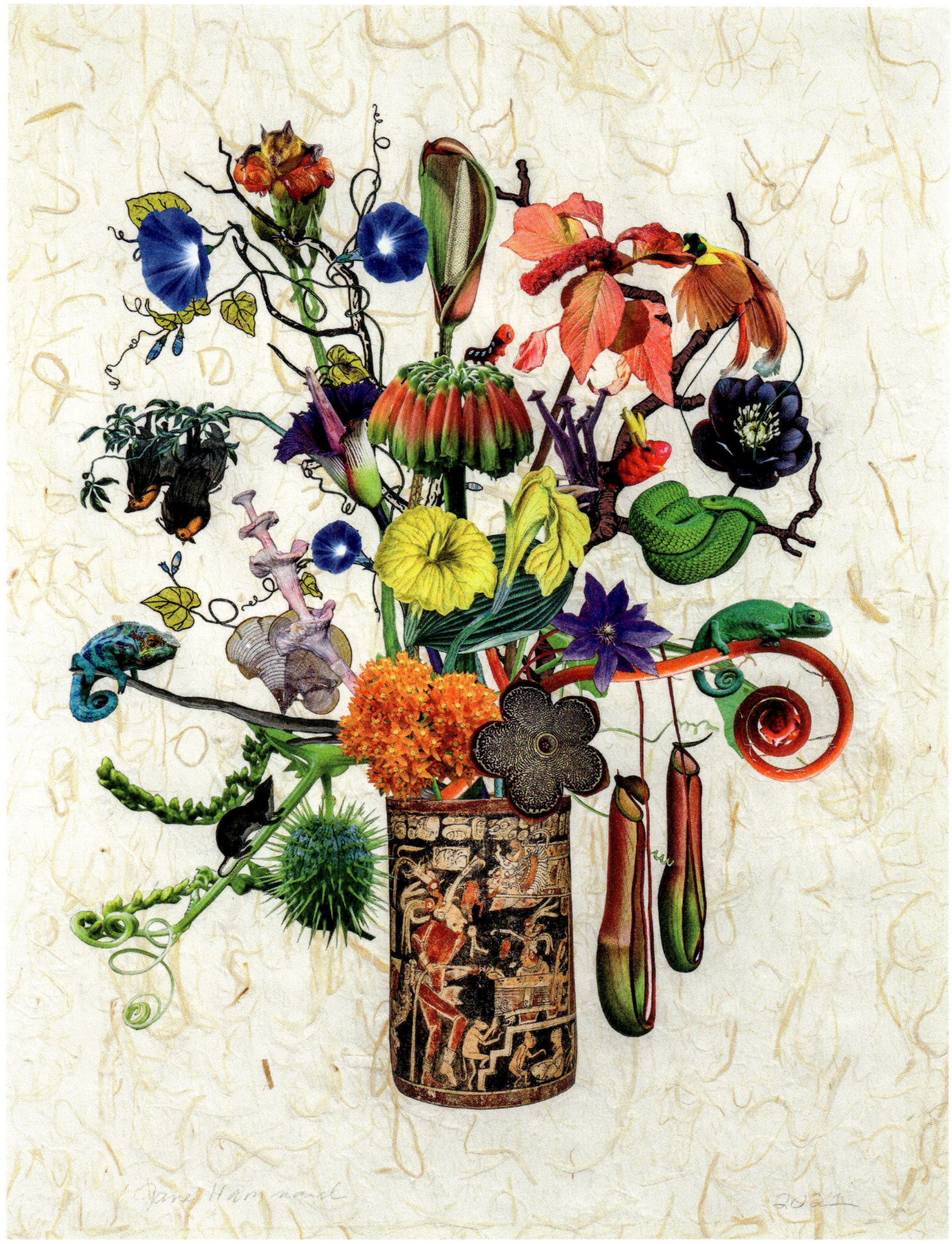

Mayan Cylinder with Green Mamba, Sphinx Moth Caterpillar and Bird of Paradise, 2021
Unique botanical collage using linocut, relief printing, digital printing, coloured pencil, Sumi ink, watercolour and gouache, hand cut and assembled on collaged Japanese papers over cotton rag
127 × 96.5 cm
50 × 38 in

Roman Glass with Bleeding Heart, Chrysanthemum and Ivy, 2024
Unique botanical collage using digital printing, coloured pencil, Sumi ink, watercolour and gouache, hand cut and assembled on indigo-dyed Japanese book pages over Japanese paper over cotton rag
45.7 × 34.9 cm
18 × 13¾ in

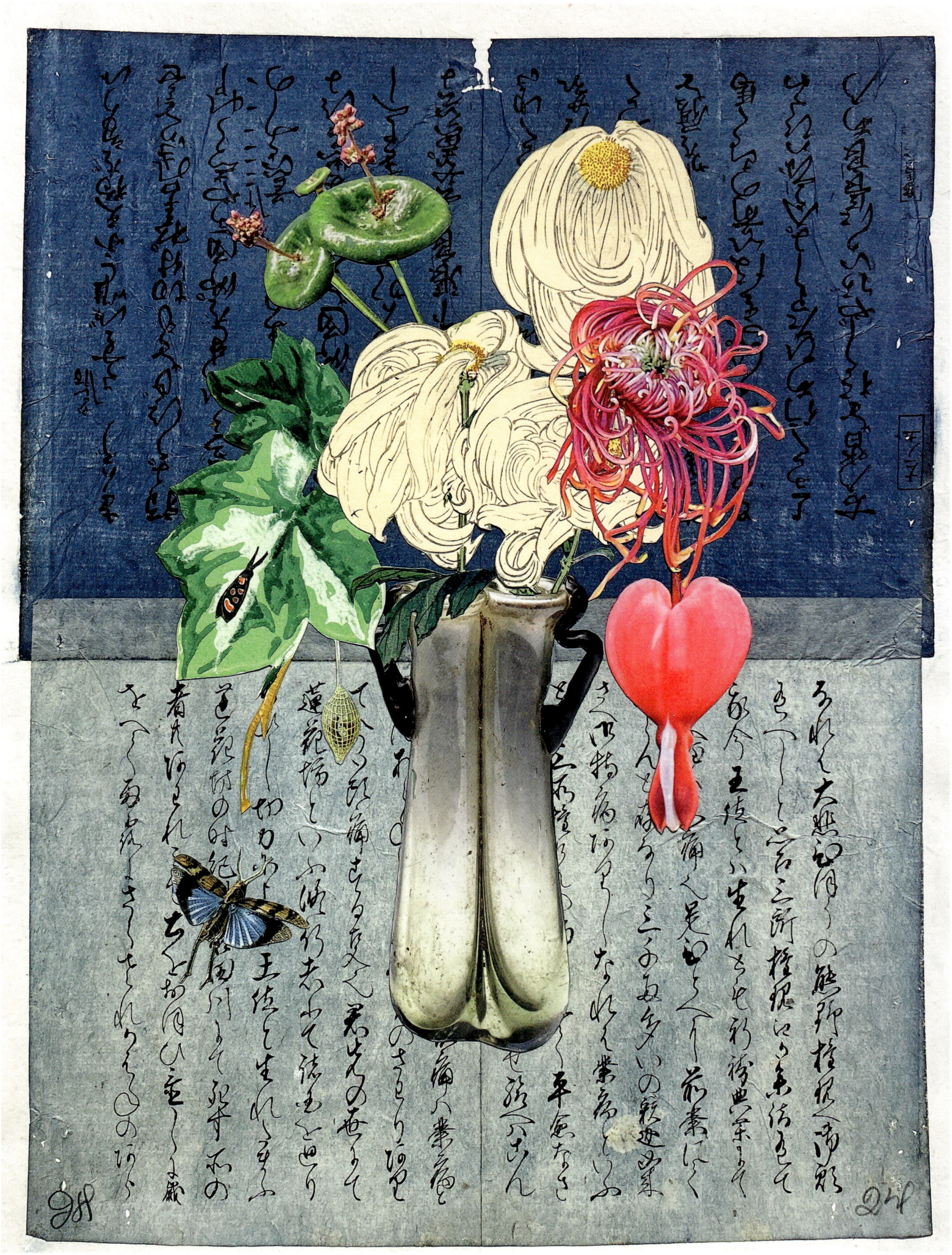

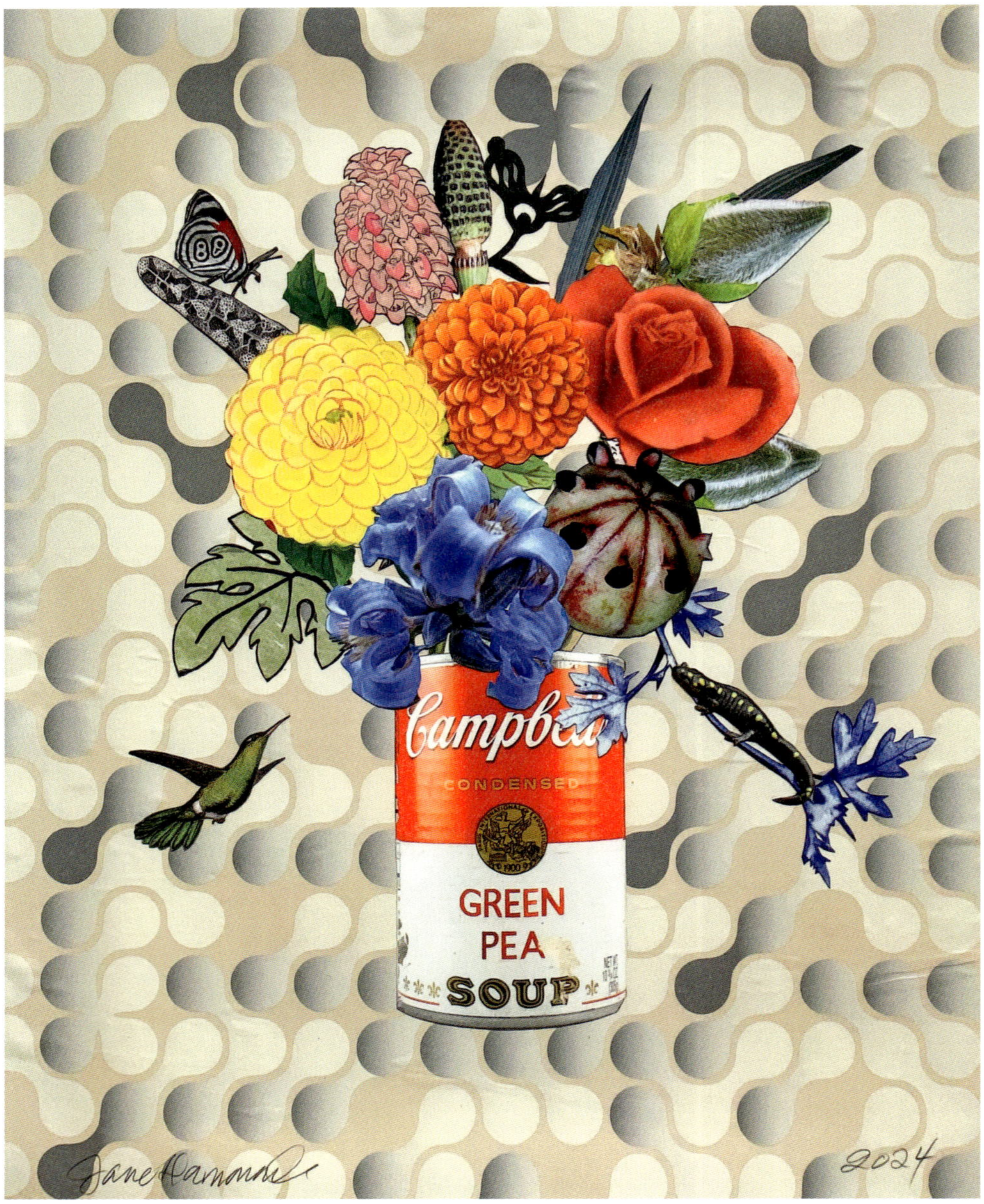

Campbell's Green Pea Soup with Borage, Spotted Salamander and Anna's Eighty-Eight, 2024
Unique botanical collage with relief printing, digital printing, coloured pencil, watercolour and gouache, hand cut and assembled on silk-screened Indian paper collaged over cotton rag
45.7 × 36.8 cm
18 × 14½ in

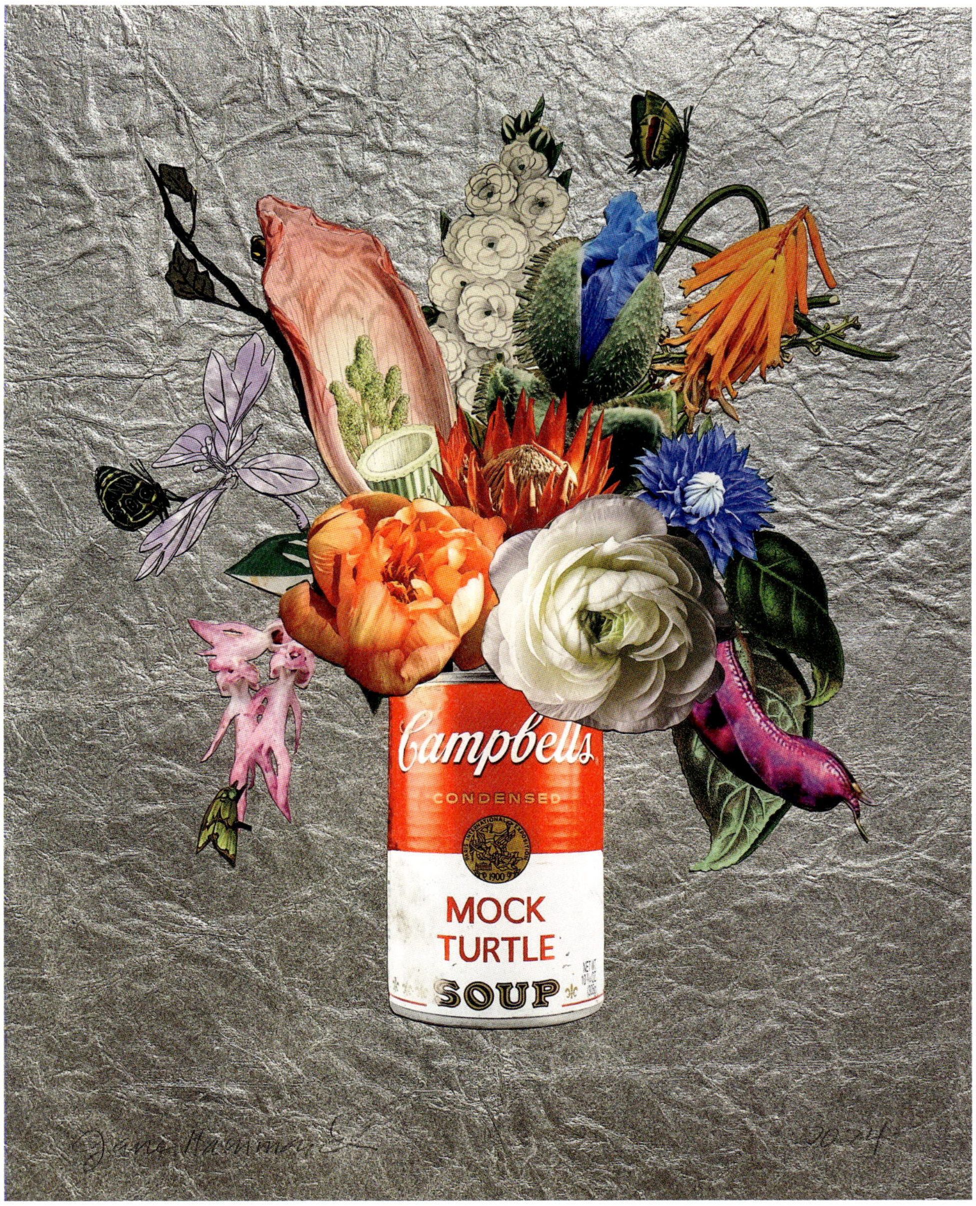

Campbell's Mock Turtle Soup with Protea, Peony and Hyacinth Beans, 2024
Unique botanical collage with relief printing, linocut, digital printing, coloured pencil, watercolour and gouache, hand cut and assembled on Nepali paper collaged over cotton rag
45.7 × 36.8 cm
18 × 14½ in

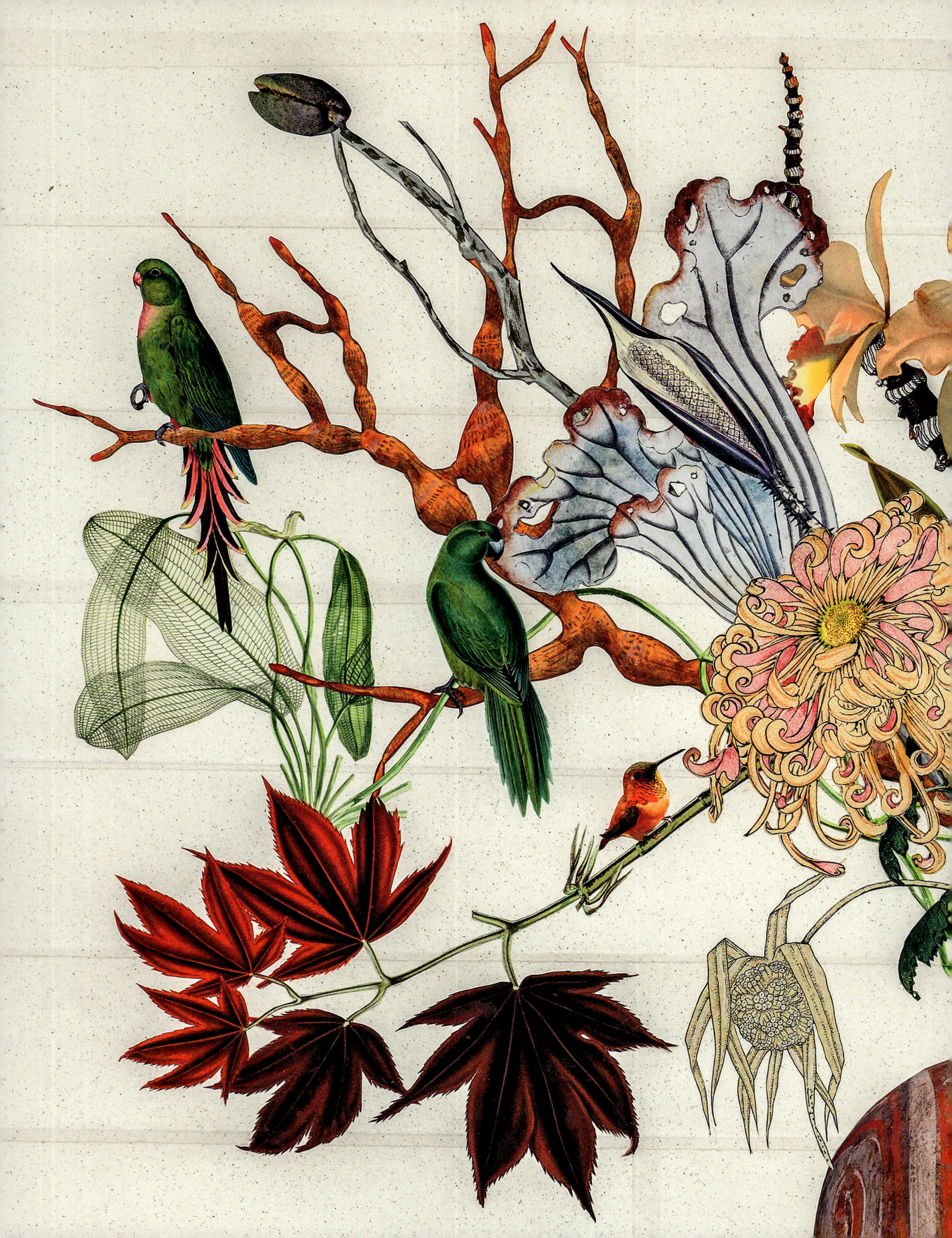

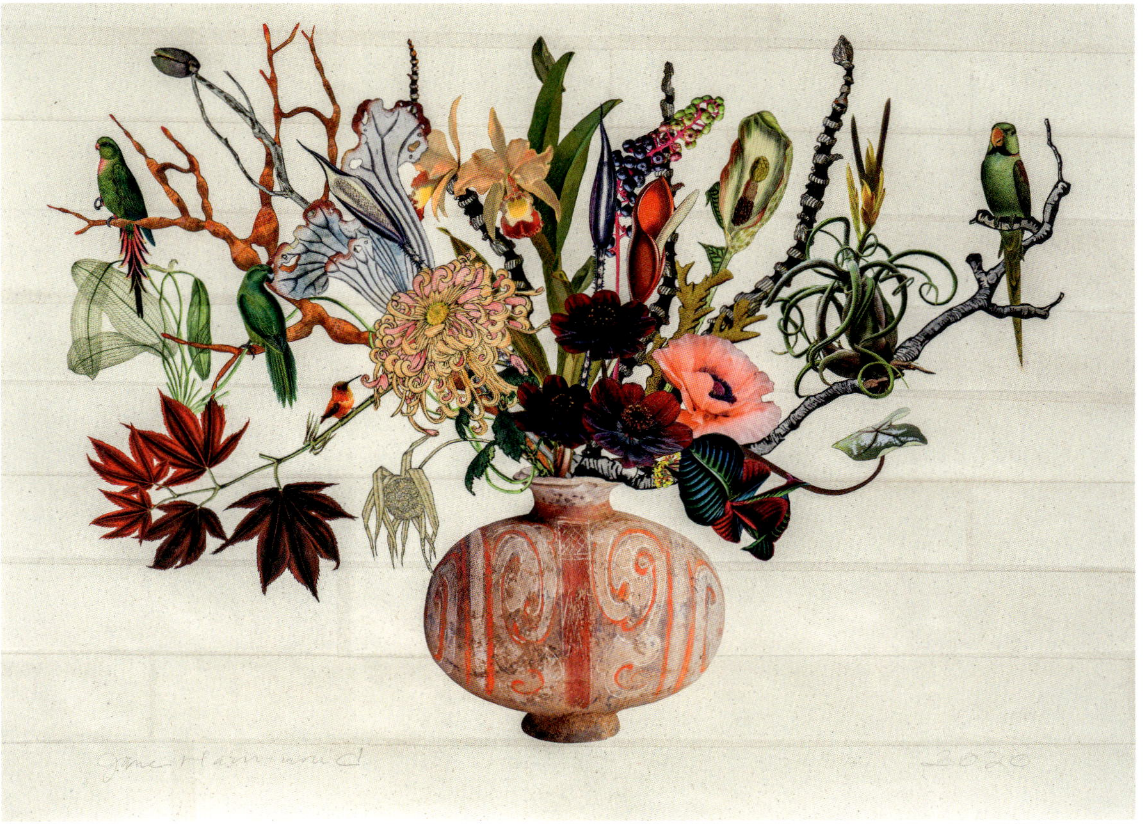

Han Dynasty Cocoon Jar with Chocolate Cosmos, Roseate Parakeet and Blushing Philodendron, 2020
Unique botanical collage using linocut, relief printing, digital printing, coloured pencil, Sumi ink, watercolour and gouache, hand cut and assembled on collaged Japanese papers over cotton rag
91.4 × 127 cm
36 × 50 in

Wedgewood Jasperware Vase with Rosy Parachutes, Nigella and Sulphur-Crested Cockatoo, 2025
Unique botanical collage using linocut, digital printing, coloured pencil, Sumi ink, watercolour and gouache, hand cut and assembled on collaged Japanese papers over cotton rag with graphite
127 × 139.7 cm
50 × 55 in

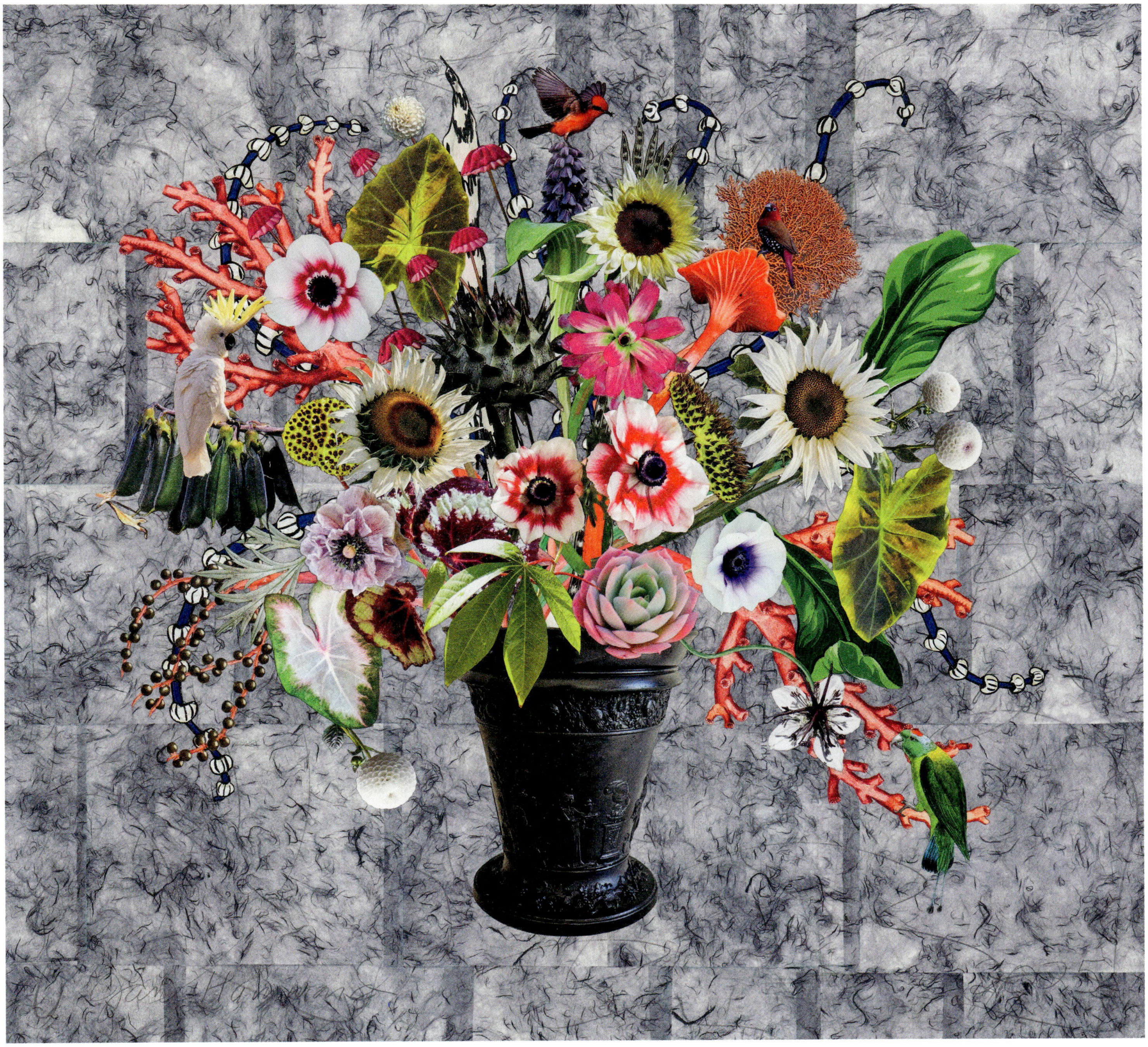

Roman Glass with Prairie Anemone, Naked Man Orchid and Pygmy Owl, 2022
Unique botanical collage using relief printing, digital printing, coloured pencil, Sumi ink, watercolour and gouache, hand cut and assembled on collaged Japanese papers over painted cotton rag
127 × 96.5 cm
50 × 38 in

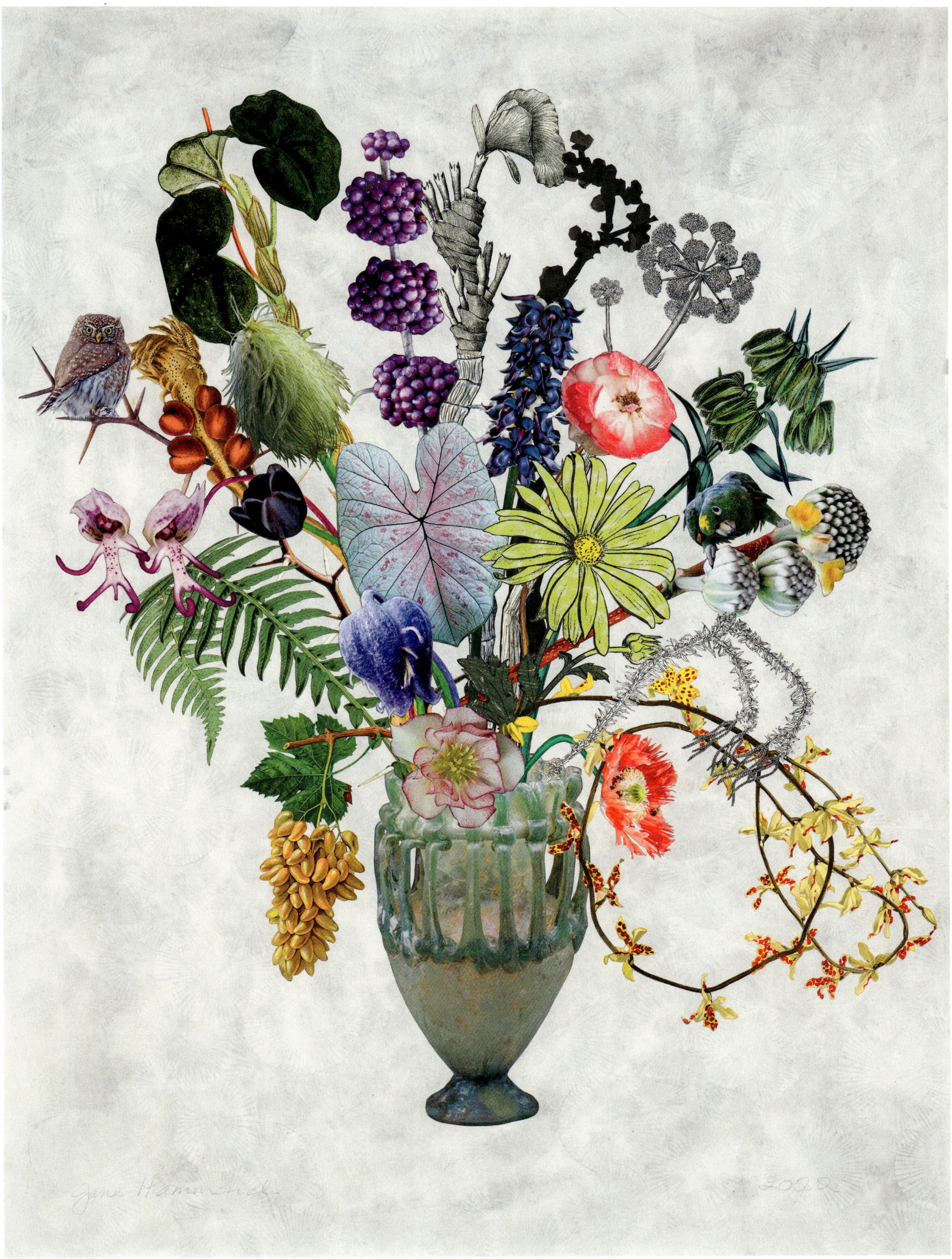

Hong Kong Vase with Monkey Face Orchid, Morning Glory and Flicker, 2017
Unique botanical collage using lithography, linocut, relief printing, digital printing, coloured pencil, Sumi ink, watercolour and gouache, hand cut and assembled on collaged Japanese papers over painted cotton rag
96.5 × 127 cm
38 × 50 in

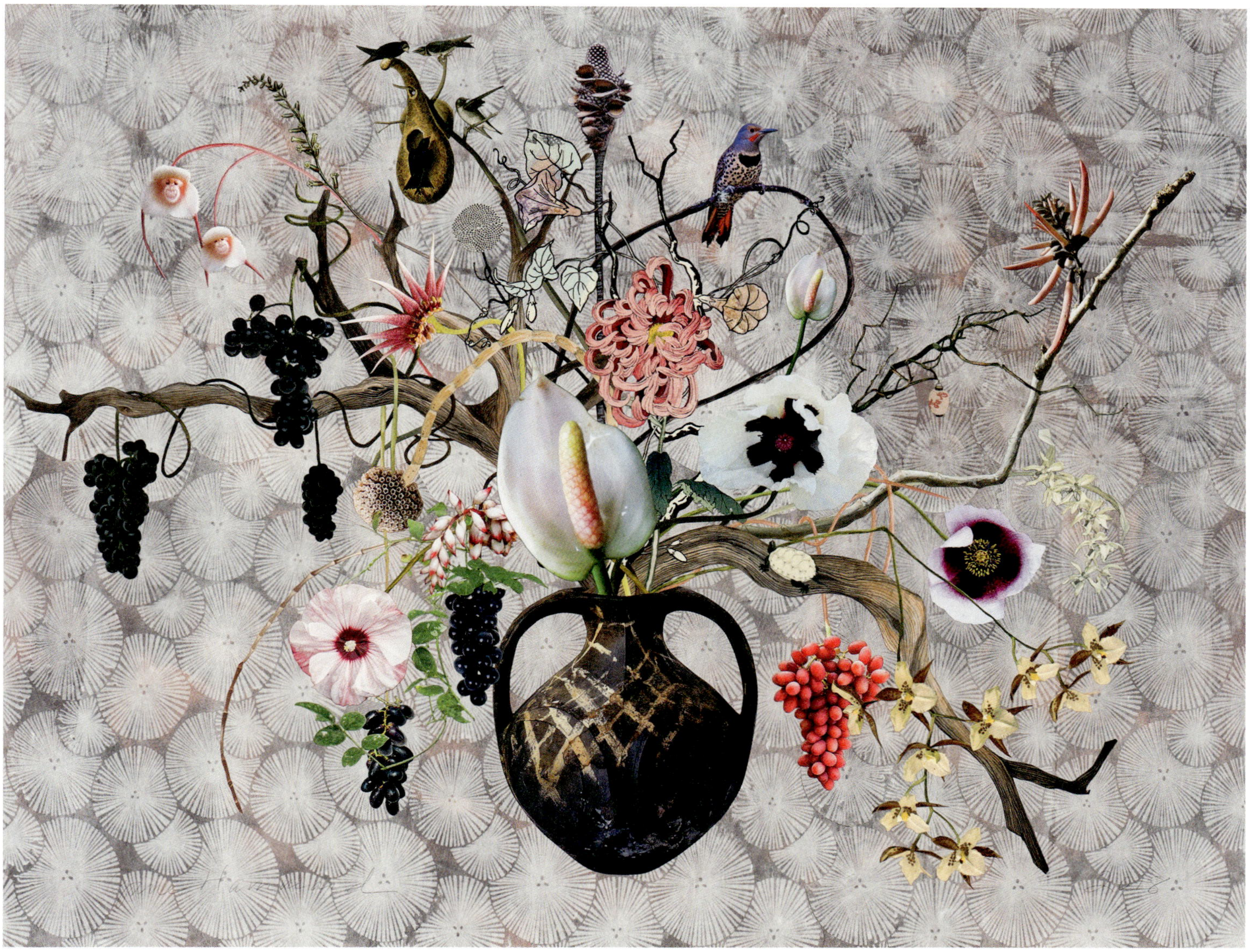

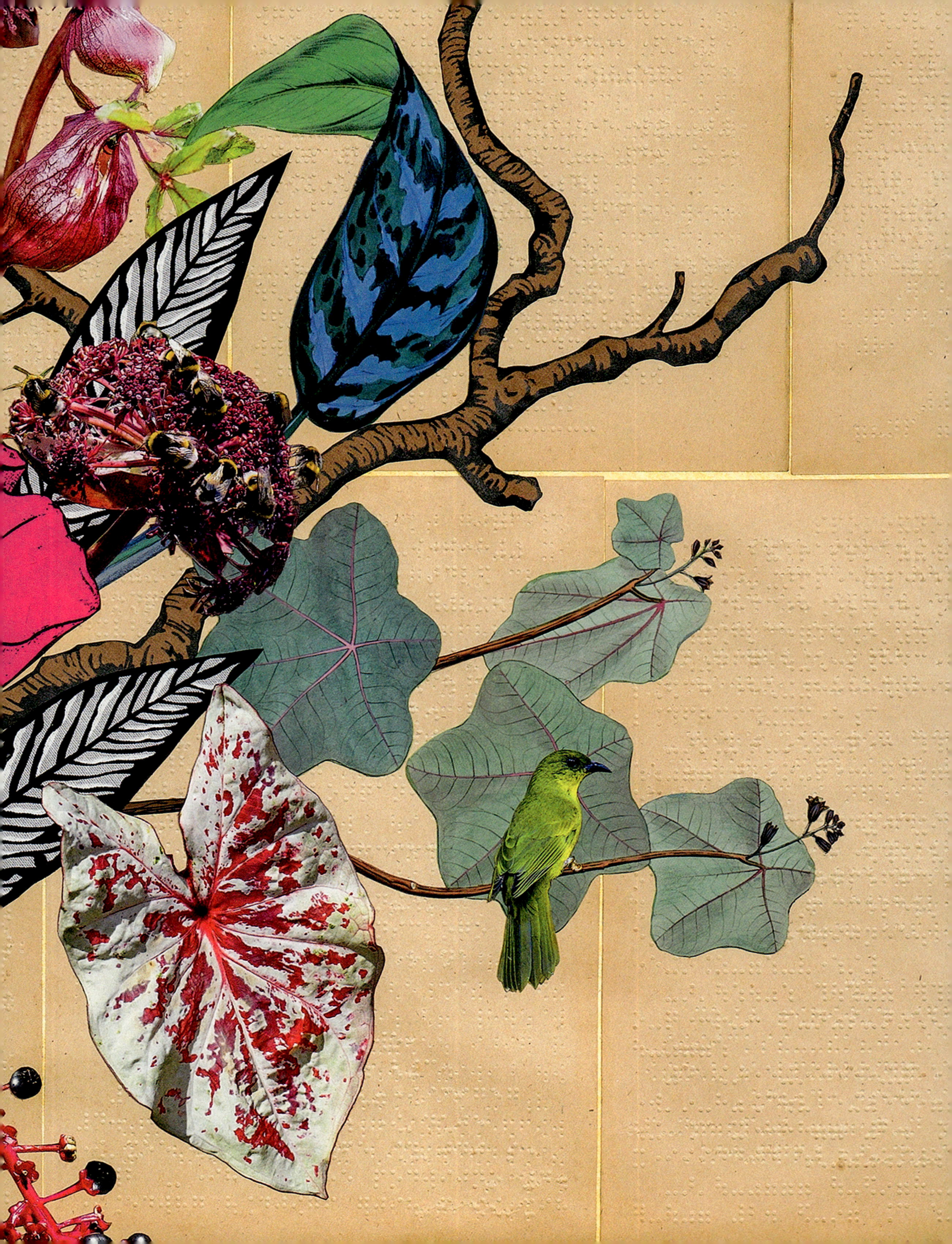

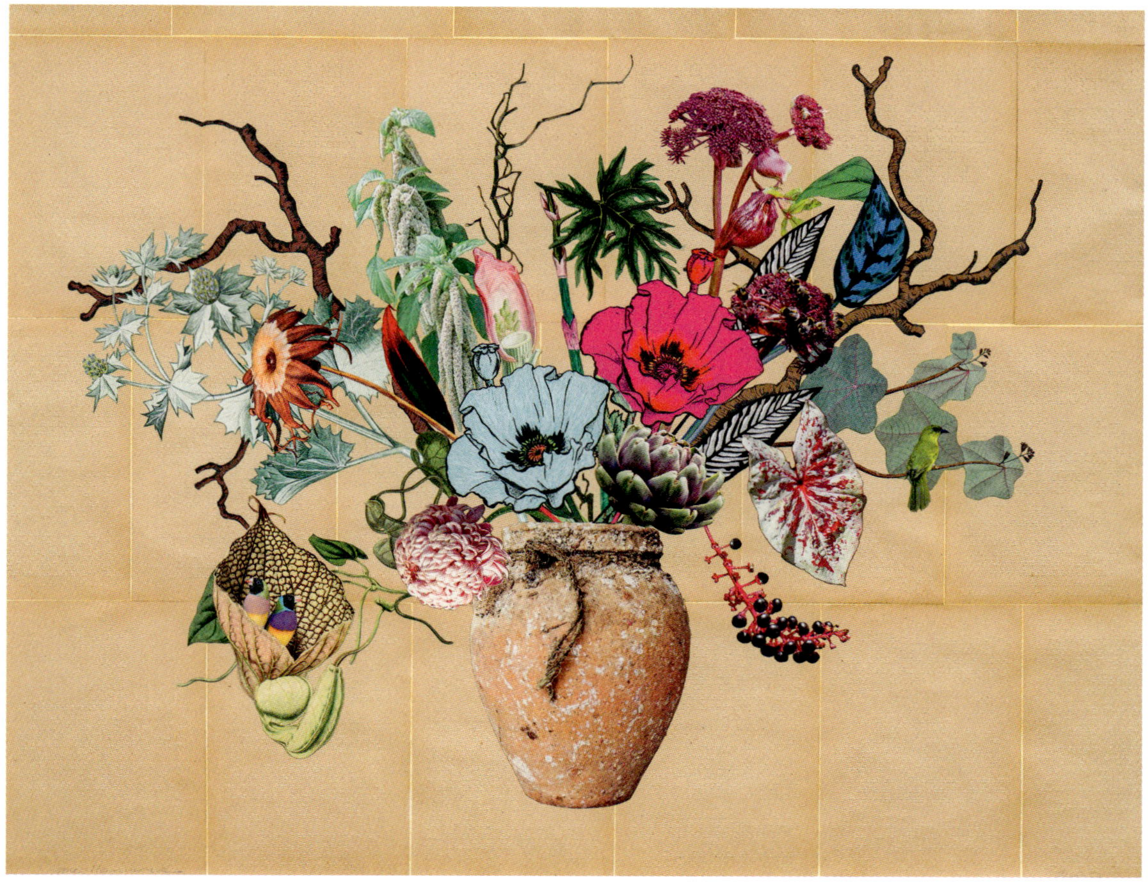

Mediterranean Octopus Trap with Pokeberries, Angelica and Dutchman's Pipe, 2022
Unique botanical collage using linocut, relief printing, digital printing, coloured pencil, Sumi ink, watercolour and gouache, hand cut and assembled on de-acidified Braille pages collaged over painted cotton rag
96.5 × 127 cm
38 × 50 in

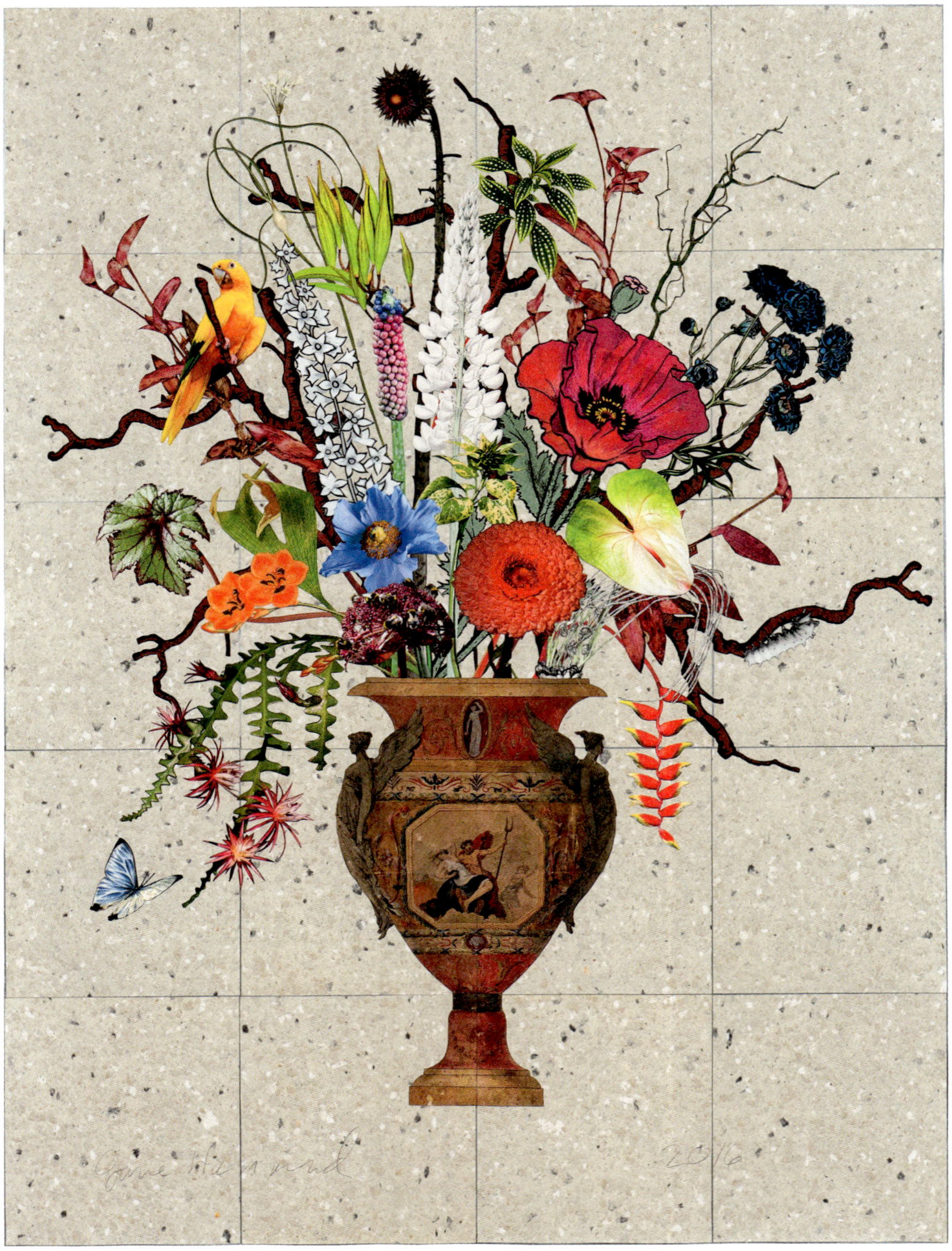

Spanish Vase with Thistle, Angelica and Lupine, 2016
Unique botanical collage using lithography, linocut, relief printing, digital printing, coloured pencil, Sumi ink, watercolour, gouache and gold leaf, hand cut and assembled on Japanese papers over painted cotton rag
127 × 96.5 cm
50 × 38 in

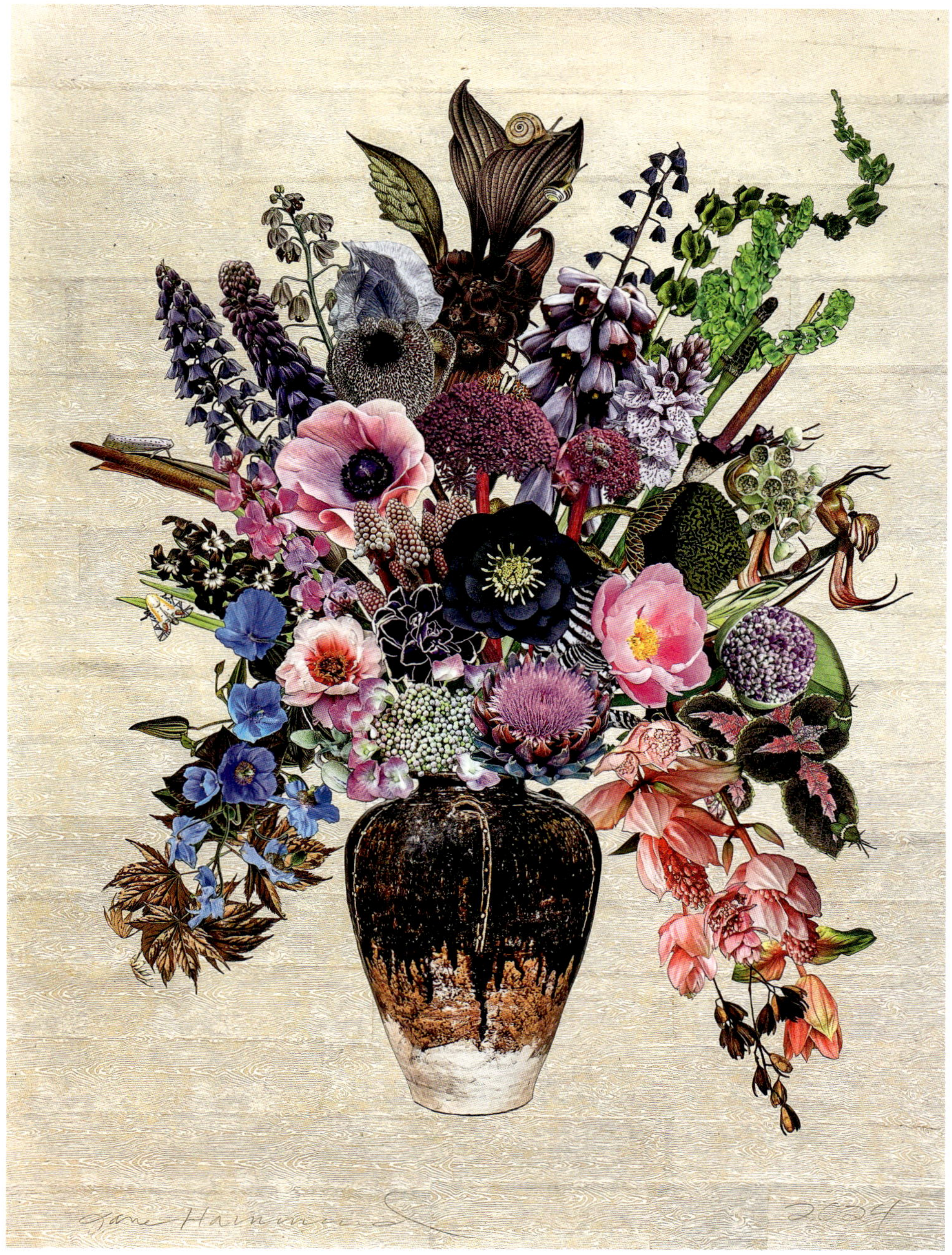

Martaban Jar with Bat Lily, Picasso Moth and Himalayan Blue Poppies, 2024
Unique botanical collage using digital printing, coloured pencil, Sumi ink, watercolour and gouache, hand cut and assembled on collaged Nepali papers over cotton rag
127 × 96.5 cm
50 × 38 in

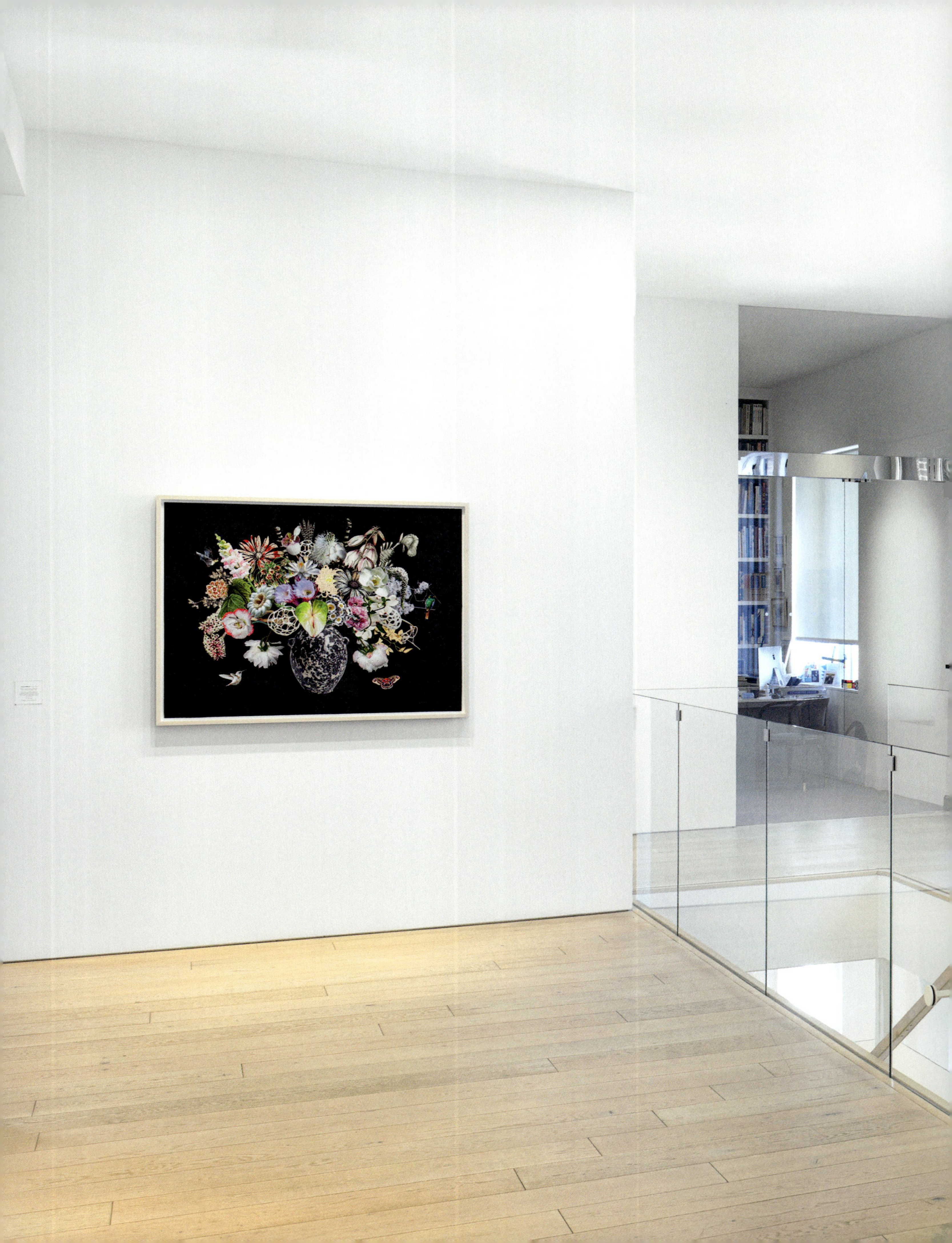

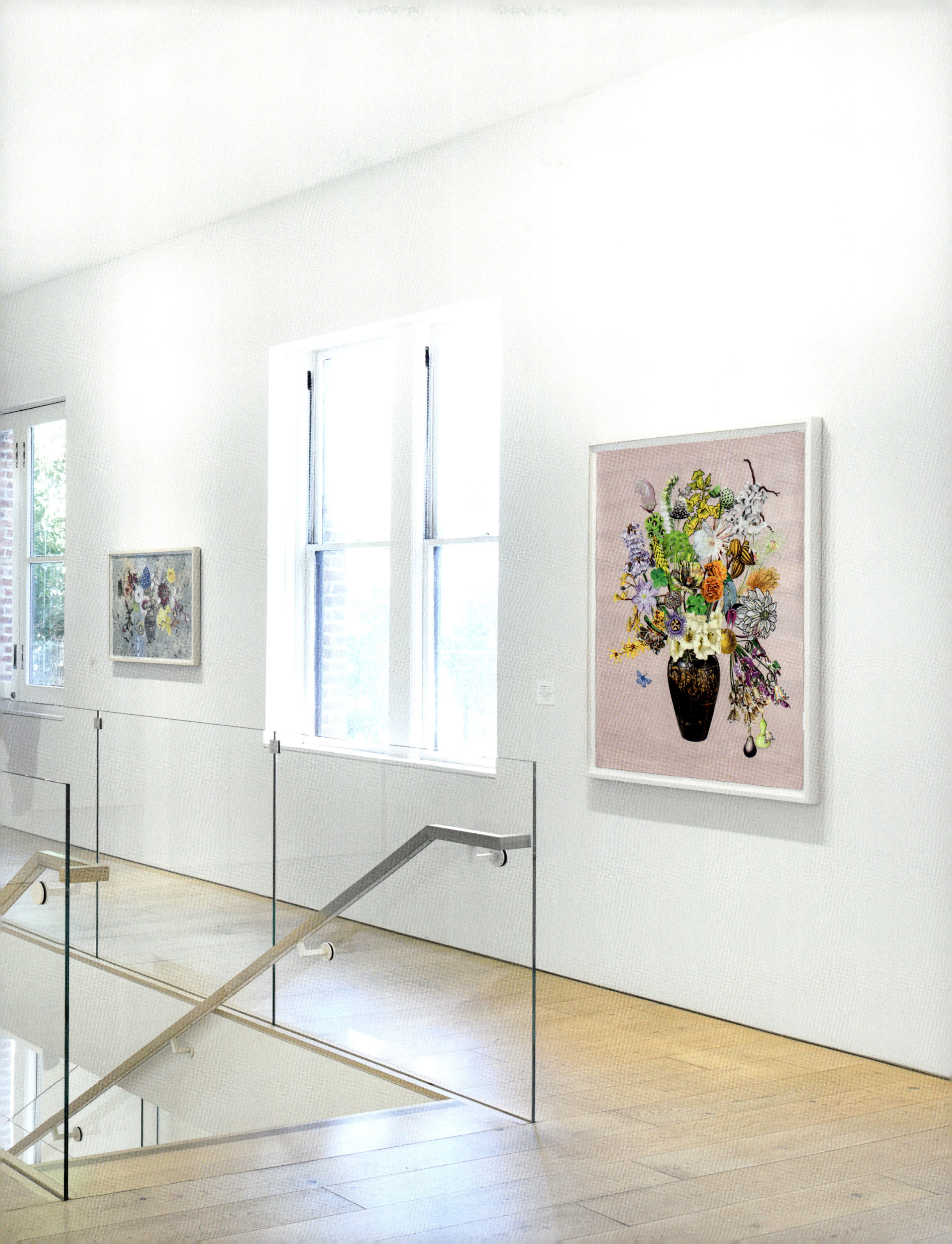

Persian Cameo Glass with Blue Macaw, Monster Beans and Monkey Puzzle Tree, 2025
Unique botanical collage using relief printing, linocut, digital printing, coloured pencil, Sumi ink, watercolour and gouache, hand cut and assembled on collaged Japanese papers over cotton rag
127 × 96.5 cm
50 × 38 in

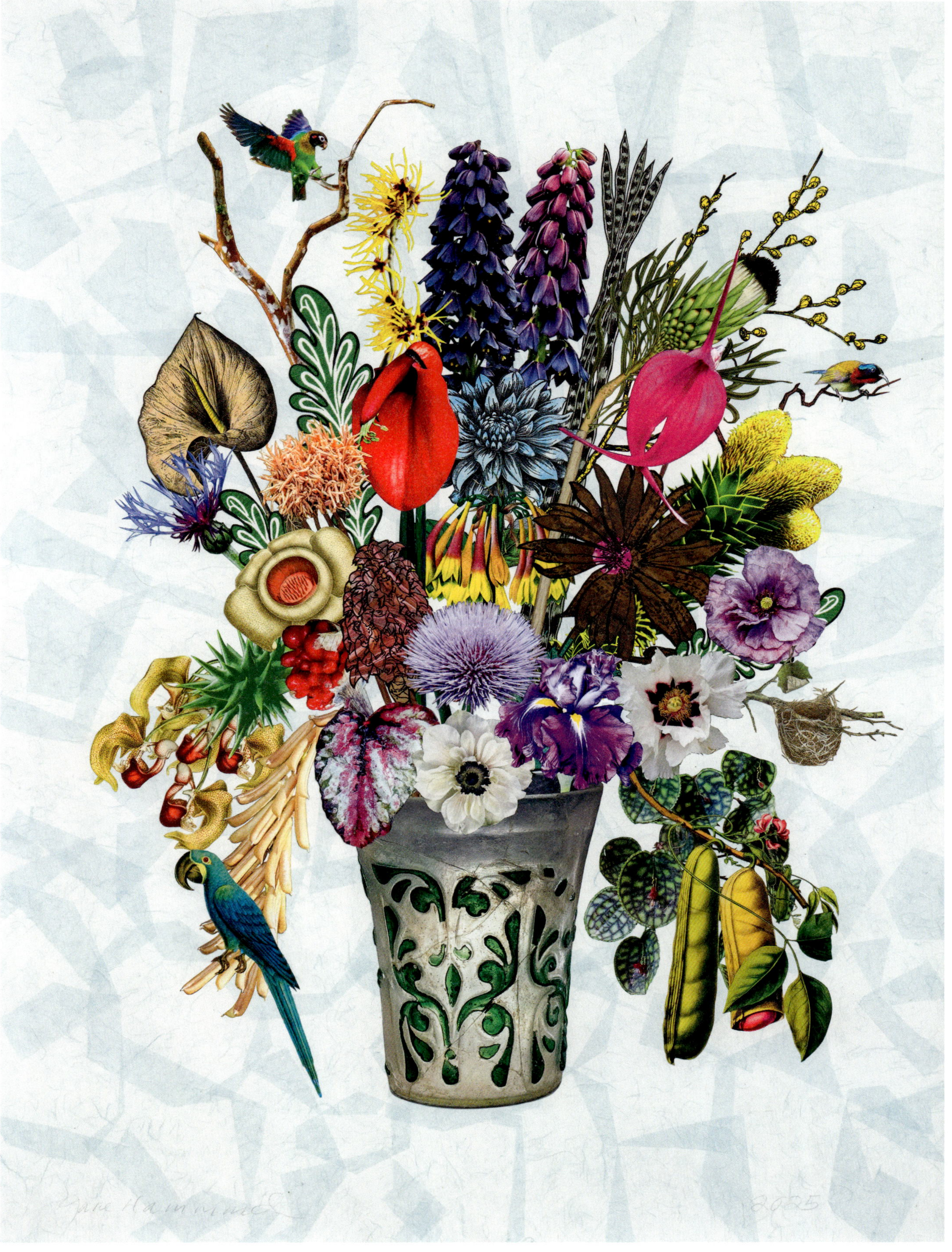

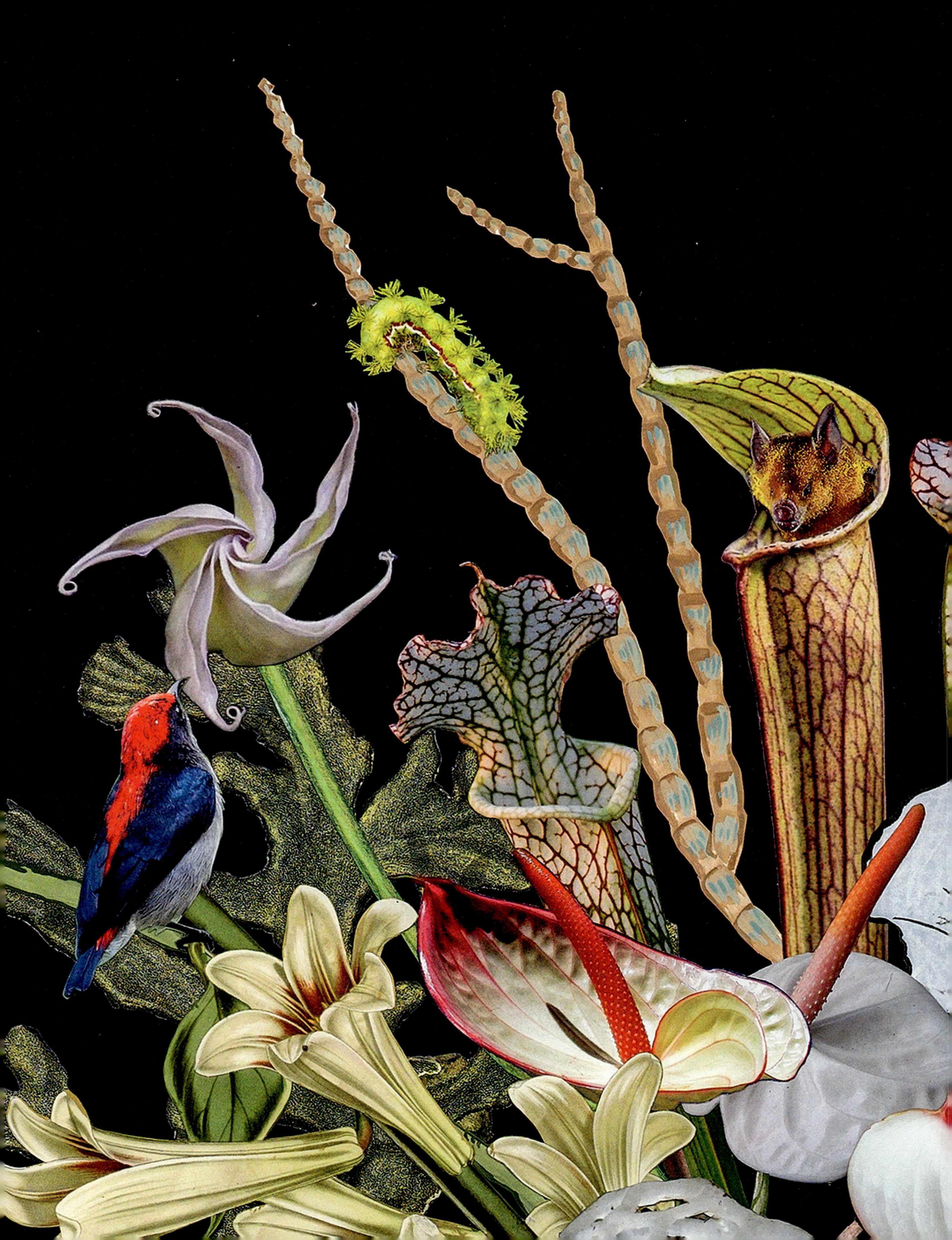

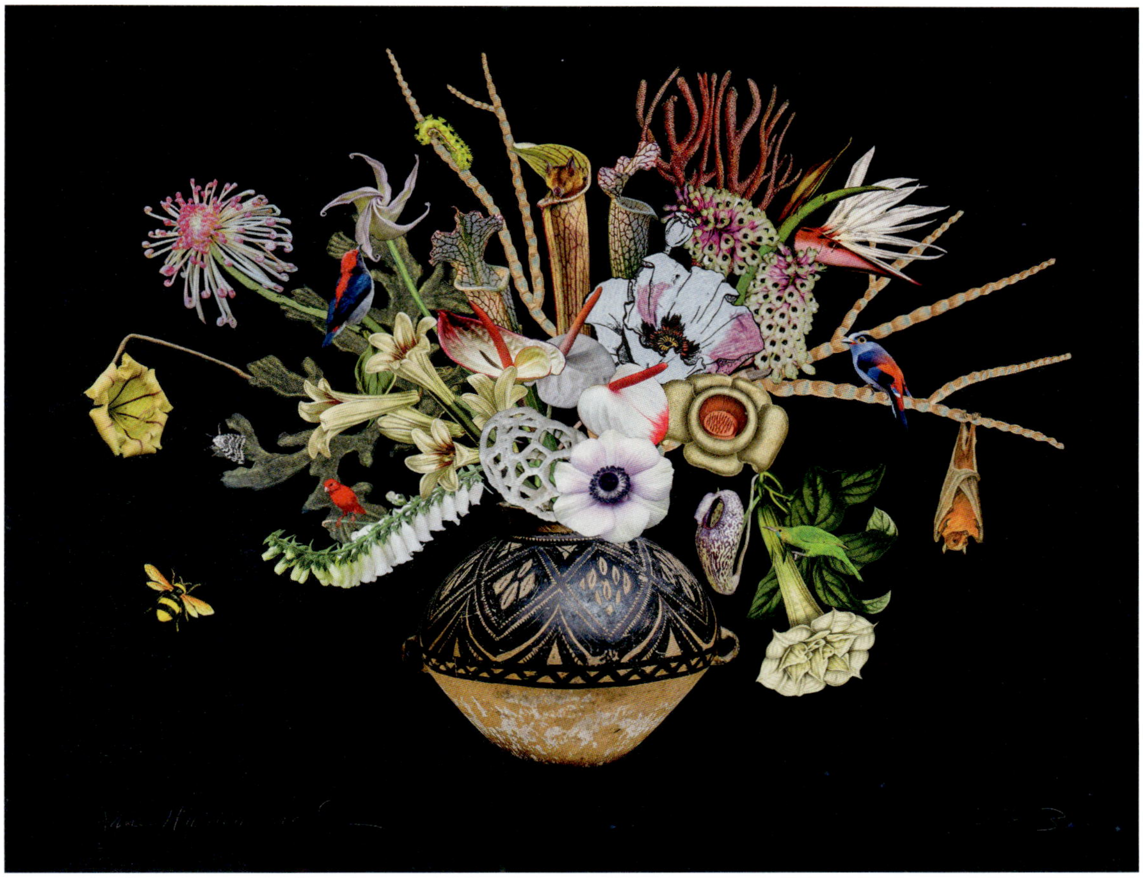

Chinese Neolithic Jar with Scarlet-Backed Flower Pecker, Pitcher Plant and Datura, 2023
Unique botanical collage using relief printing, digital printing, coloured pencil, Sumi ink, watercolour and gouache, hand cut and assembled on collaged Nepali papers over cotton rag
96.5 × 127 cm
38 × 50 in

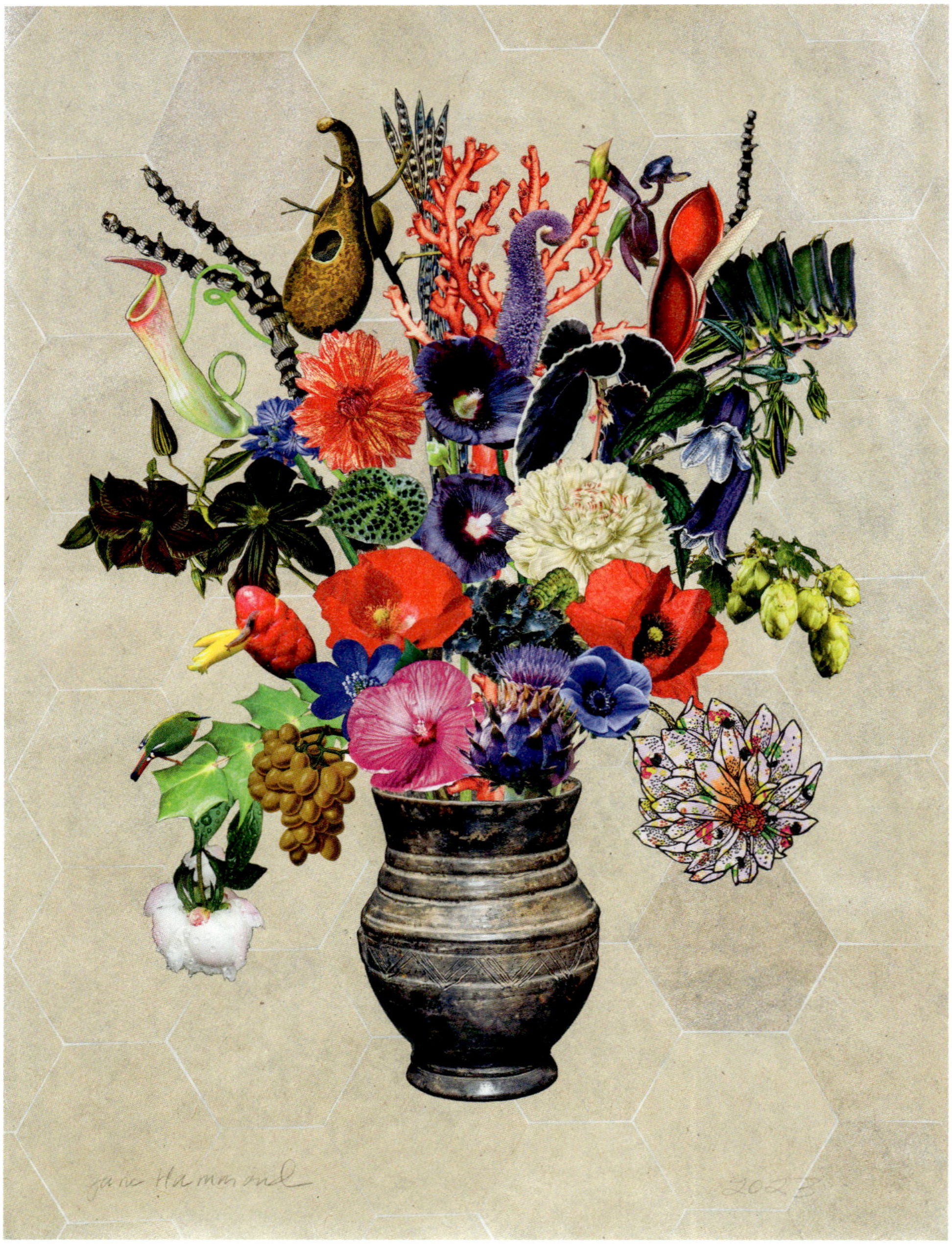

Shang Dynasty Vase with Laughing Duck Orchid, Lily of the Nile and Clematis Jackmani, 2023
Unique botanical collage using relief printing, digital printing, coloured pencil, Sumi ink, watercolour and gouache, hand cut and assembled on collaged Nepali papers with glitter over painted cotton rag
127 × 96.5 cm
50 × 38 in

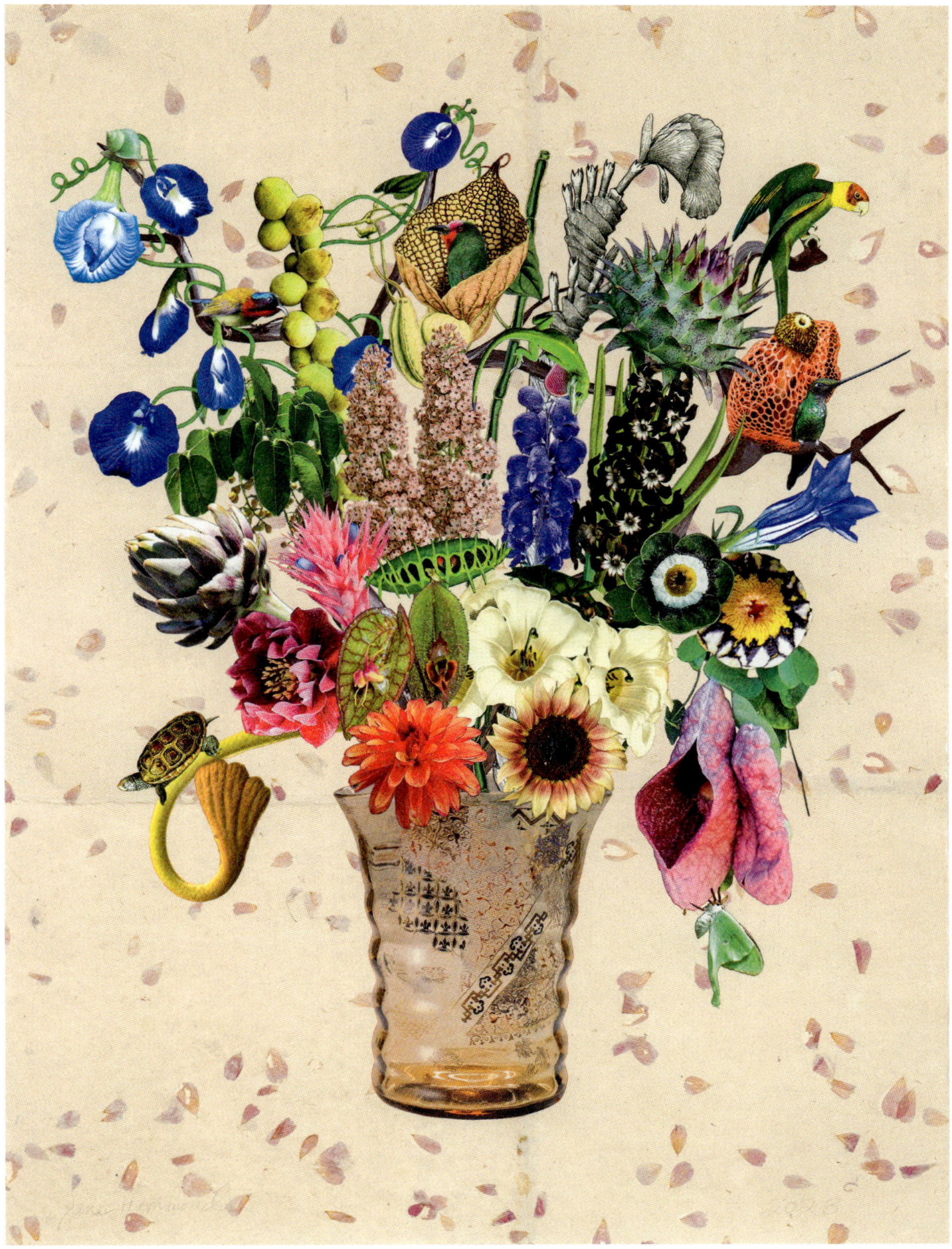

Emile Galle Vase with Aristolochia, Sword-Billed Hummingbird and Monkshood, 2023
Unique botanical collage using digital printing, coloured pencil, Sumi ink, watercolour and gouache, hand cut and assembled on collaged Bhutanese papers with Bougainvillea flowers over cotton rag
127 × 96.5 cm
50 × 38 in

Roman Glass with Long-Tailed Sylph, Himalayan Blue Poppies and Primrose, 2023
Unique botanical collage using digital printing, coloured pencil, Sumi ink, watercolour, gouache and copper leaf, hand cut and assembled on collaged Japanese papers over cotton rag
96.5 × 127 cm
38 × 50 in

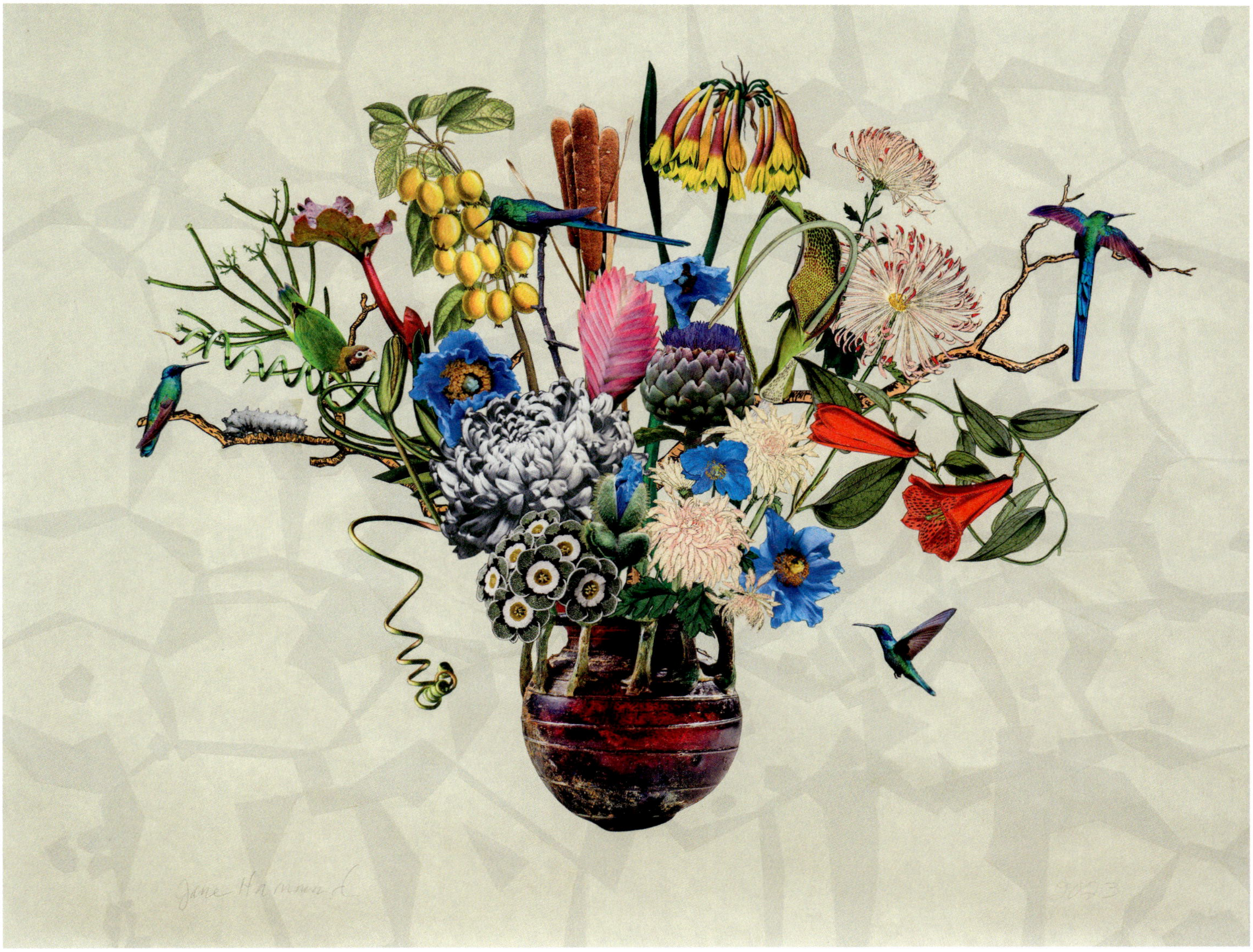

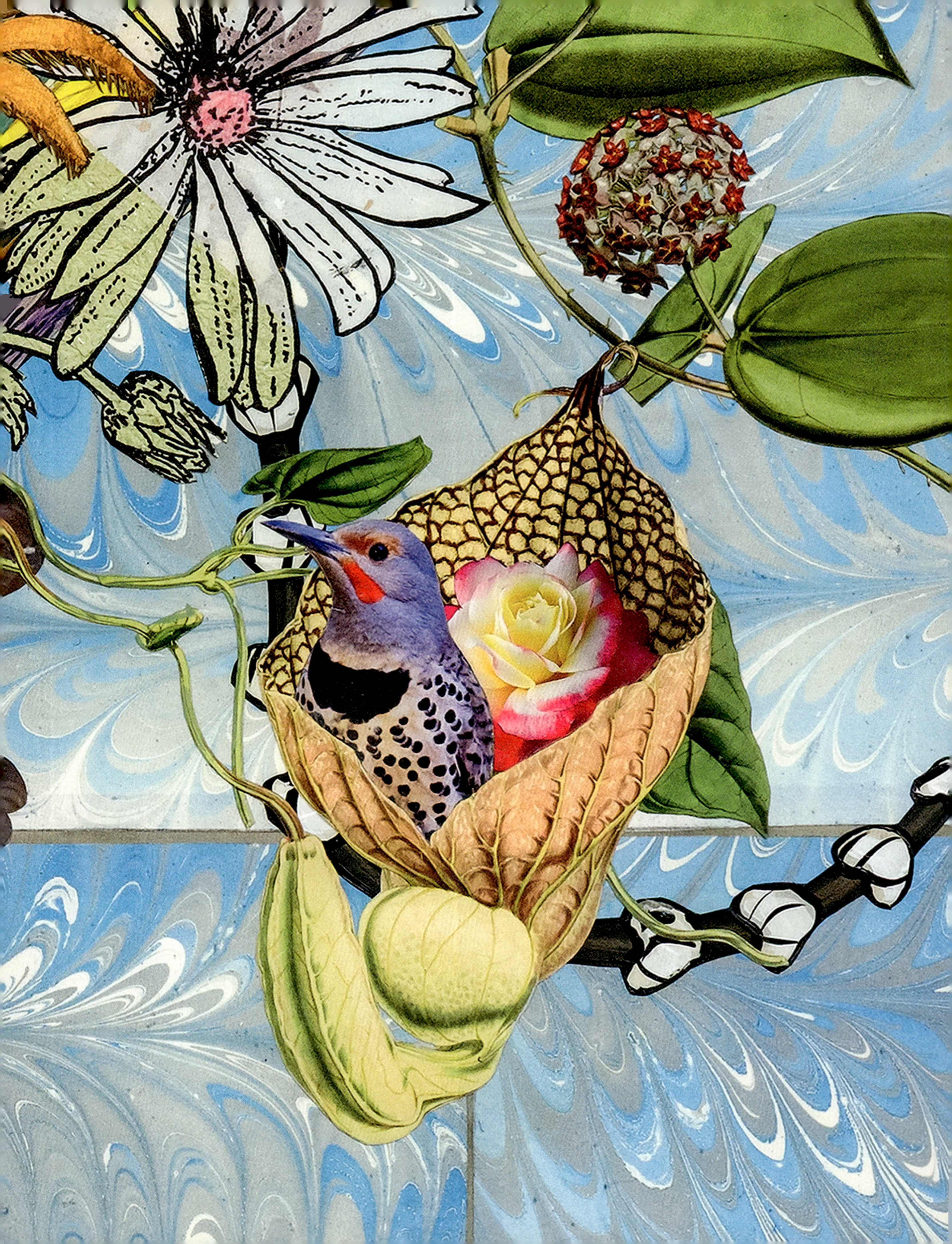

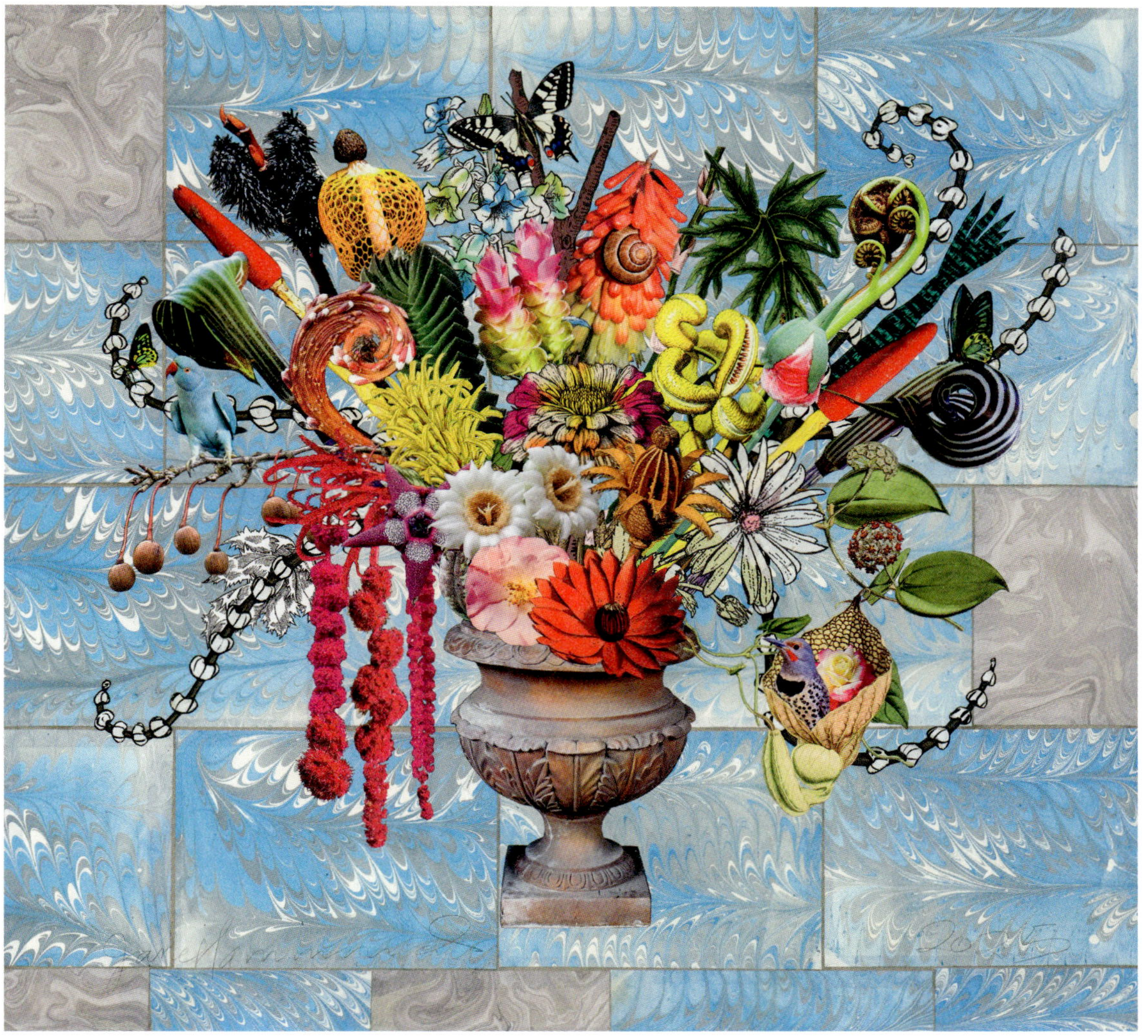

Bronze Garden Urn with Tree Fern, Jack-in-the-Pulpit and Northern Flicker, 2025
Unique botanical collage using relief printing, linocut, digital printing, coloured pencil, Sumi ink, watercolour and gouache, hand cut and assembled on collaged Indian marbled papers over painted cotton rag
127 × 139.7 cm
50 × 55 in

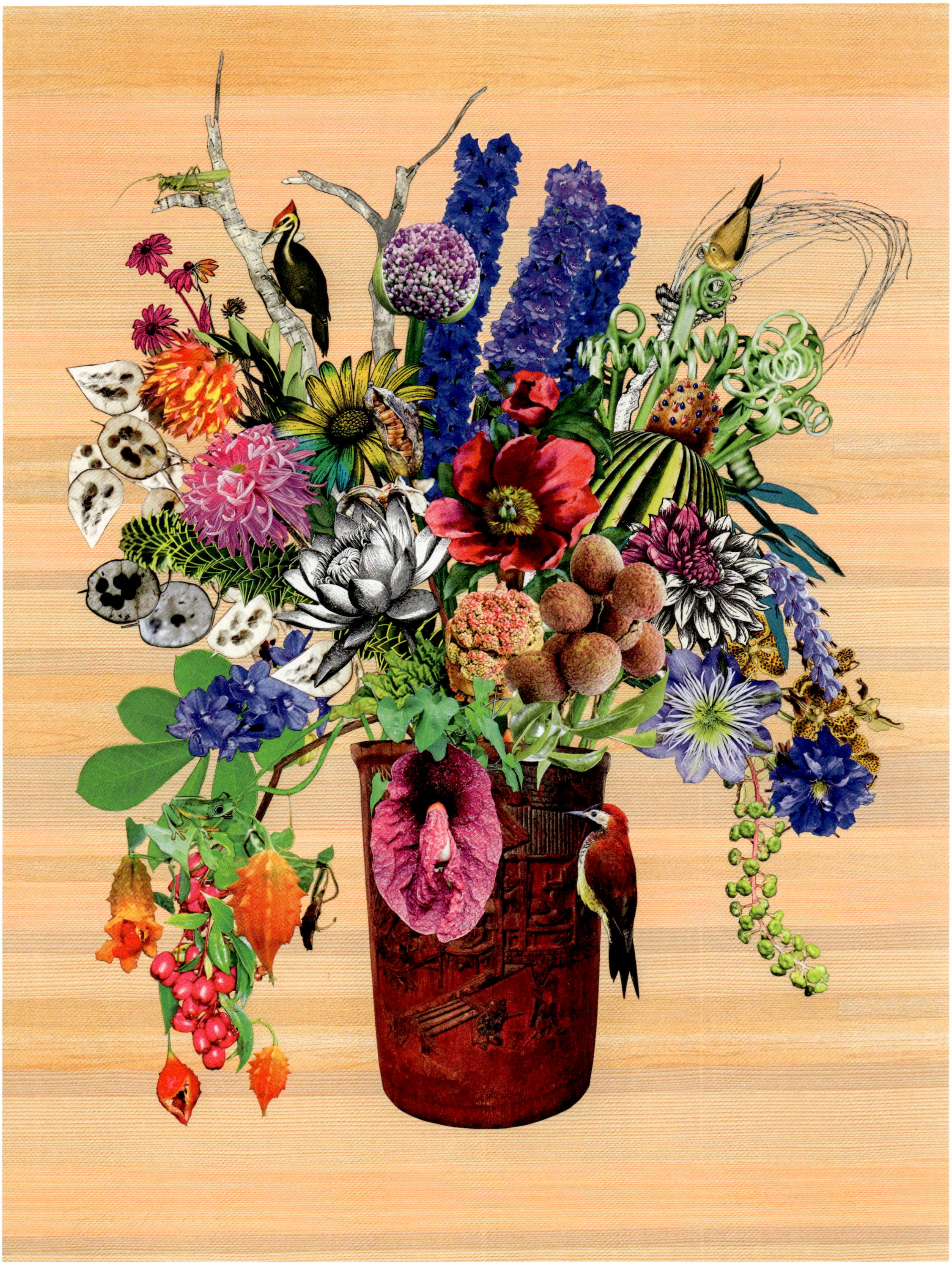

Chinese Carved Bucket with Rhubarb Flower, Grasshopper and Clematis Crystal Fountain, **2025**
Unique botanical collage using relief printing, digital printing, coloured pencil, Sumi ink, watercolour and gouache, hand cut and assembled on collaged Japanese woodgrain papers over cotton rag
127 × 96.5 cm
50 × 38 in

Gathering
Jane Hammond

Homo sapiens emerged about 300,000 years ago. They began domesticating plants and animals about 10,000 years ago. This leaves about 290,000 years between the birth of our collective ancestors and the dawn of agriculture.

This is 290,000 years of hunting and gathering. No matter what human sub-group you might identify with now, this lies in all of our pasts. What exactly is hunting and gathering? Well, hunting, which includes fishing, is the pursuit of animals that are largely mobile. And gathering is the pursuit of plants which are largely stationary. One doesn't gather rabbits, nor spear blueberries.

To touch on my own biography, when I was a child I hunted and fished with my grandfather. Always accompanying us was his beloved field trial spaniel, Ike, whose name situates us squarely in the fifties. We went for birds, pheasant mostly, and we fished for trout. Occasionally we would duck-hunt in the Sound and my grandmother would pluck the wild ducks, singe them with a match, then soak them in changes of milk to withdraw the salt.

Back to the hunt. I can say with some confidence that we were successful about half the time. Decent odds, but not great. Of course, game was more plentiful thousands of years ago, probably even vastly better than a stocked game reserve, but the offset is that the weapons of long ago were cruder.

Such so-so hunting odds point to the primacy of gathering. Between periods of those delectable feasts of deer and rabbits, grouse and buffalo, people lived on plants. They ate the roots and tubers, the stems and branches, the leaves, the fruit, the berries, the nuts and the seeds.

Plants are stationary but they're not defenceless. One survival strategy is poison. Some plants will kill you, some will just make you sick. And through the intricacies of mimicry, some plants will pretend to be poisonous by closely resembling those that are.

Early on our forebears must have learned that one cannot eat plants mindlessly. And so they developed, over thousands of years, the minds for plant-eating.

Plant-eating requires a certain kind of focused attention and sophisticated cognition and it rewards those who develop it with life itself. Look closely at these purple berries – are they the same delicious berries we gorged on by the river last week or are they the berries that poisoned my brother the week before?

Are they the same bluish purple? Is the berry the same

shape? The same shininess or does it have a dusty mask? Are they dangling in clumps? How do they affix to the branch? And the leaves of the plant, are they round like the moon? Pointy like an arrowhead? Divided like the fingers on my hand? There are a hundred things to notice about a plant: are the leaves oppositional or staggered? Are their edges serrated? Are the needles in pairs or triads? Do the thorns angle up or down?

People who paid deep attention to plants, who were able to observe closely and note differences, lived – to find more sustenance and refine the depth and nuance of their thought patterns yet again.

For tens of thousands of years, people looked closely at plants. They looked at plants as if their lives depended upon it. The more observationally sophisticated they became, the more their brains adapted to handle and process the observations, the gradations of colour and shape, structure and pattern, the better their odds. The attentive plant-lookers prospered. And became more attentive.

In this process lie the beginnings of compare-and-contrast thinking which is an important basis of modern analytical thought. In what ways are these two phenomena alike? In what ways are they different? Can you compare in detail two examples right in front of you now? Can you compare and contrast them over time? Can you recollect the specificities of A so clearly that you can discern in B a month later important similarities or differences? Can you begin to establish and communicate what importance actually means, what features are necessary to this decision and what are merely contingent?

If you think about it, much of intellectual history utilises this very skill set. Take Law, for example, with its scaffolding of precedent. In what ways does this new case resemble this older, already adjudicated case? In what important ways is it different?

So I submit that to think of flowers or plants in general as beautiful or interesting isn't the half of it. Our very ability to have such thoughts is their doing. They made us into who we are as sentient, sophisticated cognitive beings. And this is why the pleasure and engaged fulfilment we get from looking closely at plants is like no other. Because this looking, this very special, focused looking, made us who we are – and to be even unconsciously reminded of this makes us feel more deeply and fully human.

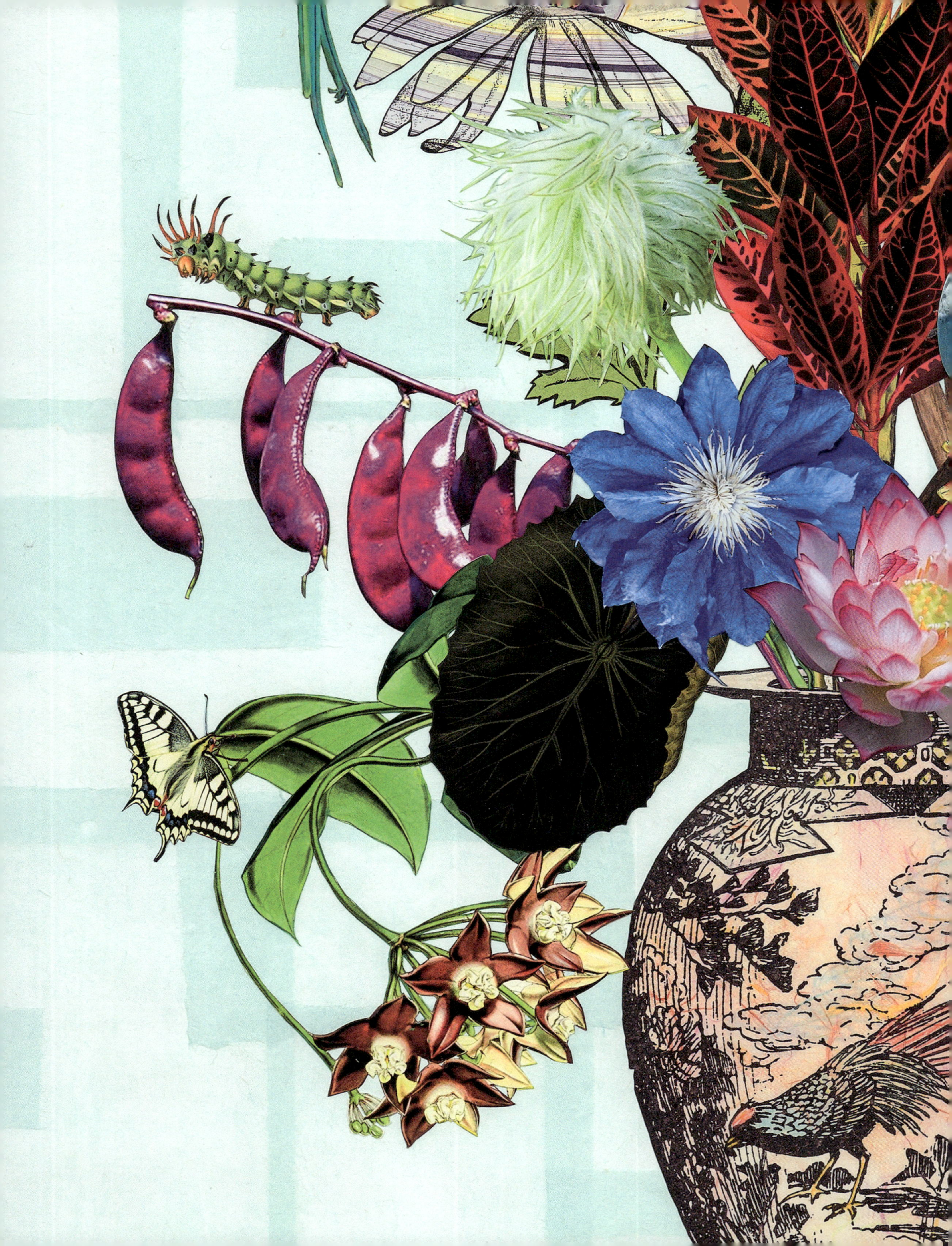

Artist Biography

Jane Hammond is an American artist who has shown regularly since the late 1980s. She has had twenty-one solo exhibitions in New York City, as well as in Paris, London, Stockholm, Barcelona, Bilbao, Amsterdam and Milan. She has also shown with galleries in Detroit, Seattle, Chicago, Kansas City, Buffalo, Los Angeles and San Francisco. She has a diverse practice and her twenty-nine solo museum exhibitions in the USA have comprised painting, works on paper, artist books, photography and sculpture. Hammond lives and works in New York City. She is represented there and in Paris by Galerie Lelong. She is represented in San Francisco by Berggruen Gallery and in London by Lyndsey Ingram Gallery.

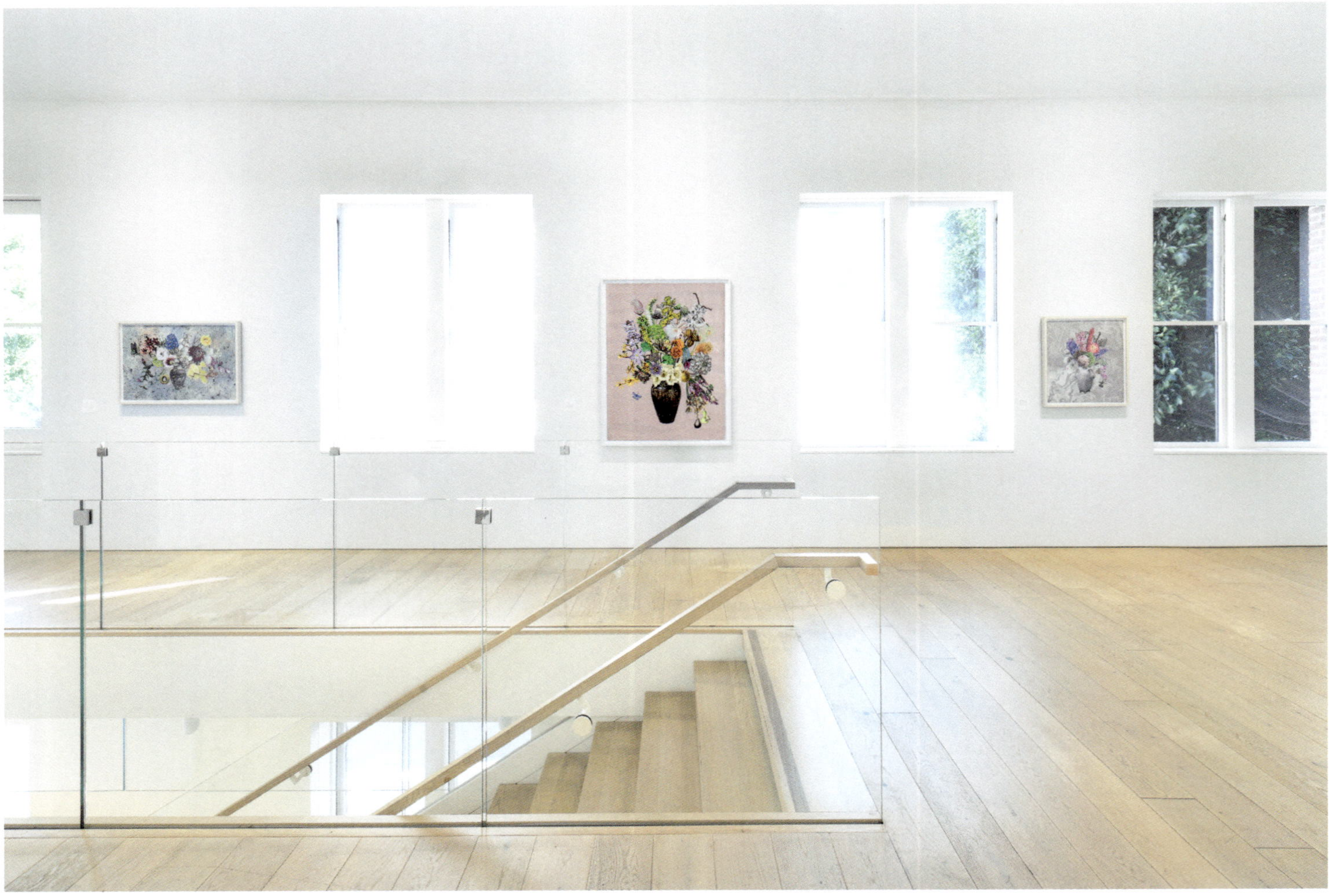

Exhibition view of ***Jane Hammond: Chocolate Cosmos, String of Pearls***
Berggruen Gallery, San Francisco
23 October 2025 – 8 January 2026

Selected Public Collections

Addison Gallery of American Art, *Andover, MA*
Albertina, *Vienna, Austria*
Aldrich Museum of Contemporary Art, *Ridgefield, CT*
Amon Carter Museum of American Art, *Fort Worth, TX*
The University of Arizona Museum of Art, *Tucson, AZ*
Arkansas Museum of Fine Arts, *Little Rock, AR*
Art, Design & Architecture Museum, *University of California, Santa Barbara, CA*
Art Institute of Chicago
Baltimore Museum of Art, *MD*
Bibliothèque Nationale, *Paris, France*
Bilbao Fine Arts Museum, *Bilbao, Spain*
Boise Art Museum, *Boise, ID*
Brooklyn Museum
Buffalo AKG Art Museum, *NY*
Carnegie Museum of Art, *Pittsburgh, PA*
Chazen Museum of Art, *University of Wisconsin, Madison*
Cincinnati Art Museum
Cleveland Museum of Art
Colby College Museum of Art, *Waterville, Maine*
The Colorado Collection, *University of Colorado at Boulder, CO*
The Contemporary Art Museum St. Louis, *MI*
The Corcoran Gallery of Art, *Washington, DC*
Cranbrook Art Museum, *Bloomfield Hills, MI*
The Detroit Institute of Arts
The deYoung Museum, *San Francisco, CA*
Flint Institute of Arts, *Flint, MI*
The Fogg Art Museum, *Harvard University*
Fort Wayne Museum of Art, *Ft. Wayne, IN*
Grand Valley State University, *Grand Rapids, MI*
Grinnell College Museum of Art, *Grinnell, IA*
Grunewald Center for Graphic Arts, *Los Angeles, CA*
Hallie Ford Museum, *Williamette University, Salem, OR*
The Heckscher Museum of Art, *Huntington, NY*
Henry Art Gallery, *Seattle, WA*
Herbert F. Johnson Museum, *Cornell University, Ithaca, NY*
Hood Museum of Art, *Dartmouth College, Hanover, NH*
Honolulu Museum of Art, *Hawaii*
Jordan Schnitzer Museum of Art, *University of Oregon, Eugene, OR*
Joslyn Art Museum, *Omaha, NB*
J. Paul Getty Museum, *Los Angeles, CA*
Knoxville Museum of Art, *Knoxville, TN*
The Library of Congress
Madison Museum of Contemporary Art, *Madison, WI*

Maryland Institute College of Art, *Baltimore, MD*
Mead Art Museum, Amherst College, *Amherst, MA*
Metropolitan Museum of Art, *New York City*
Milwaukee Art Museum
Mount Holyoke College Art Museum, *South Hadley, MA*
Museo de Arte Contemporaneo, *Mexico City, Mexico*
Museum of Contemporary Art, *Chicago*
Museum of Contemporary Art, *San Diego*
Museum of Fine Arts, *Boston*
Museum of Fine Arts, *Houston*
Museum of Fine Arts, *St. Petersburg, FL*
Museum of Modern Art, *New York City*
National Gallery of Art, *Washington, DC*
National Museum of Women in the Arts, *Washington, DC*
Nerman Museum of Contemporary Art, *Overland Park, KS*
New York Public Library, *New York City*
Orlando Museum of Art, *Orlando, FL*
Palm Springs Art Museum, *Palm Springs, CA*
Portland Art Museum, *Portland, OR*
Princeton University Art Museum, *Princeton, NJ*
Reed College Cooley Art Gallery, *Portland, OR*
Saint Louis Art Museum, *MI*
San Francisco Museum of Modern Art
San José Museum of Art, *CA*
Scottsdale Museum of Contemporary Art, *Scottsdale, AZ*
Seattle Art Museum, *Seattle, WA*
Smith College Museum of Art, *Northampton, MA*
Smithsonian American Art Museum, *Washington, DC*
Sonoma State University, *Rohnert Park, CA*
Spencer Museum of Art, *University of Kansas, Lawrence, KS*
Syracuse University Art Museum, *Syracuse, NY*
Toledo Museum of Art, *OH*
Tucson Museum of Art, *AZ*
The Walker Art Center, *Minneapolis, MN*
Wayne State University Art Museum, *Detroit, MI*
Weatherspoon Art Museum, *The University of North Carolina, Greensboro*
Wellesley College Davis Museum and Cultural Center, *Wellesley, MA*
West Virginia University Art Museum, *Morgantown, WV*
The Whitney Museum of American Art
Williams College Museum of Art, *Williamstown, MA*
Yale University Art Museum

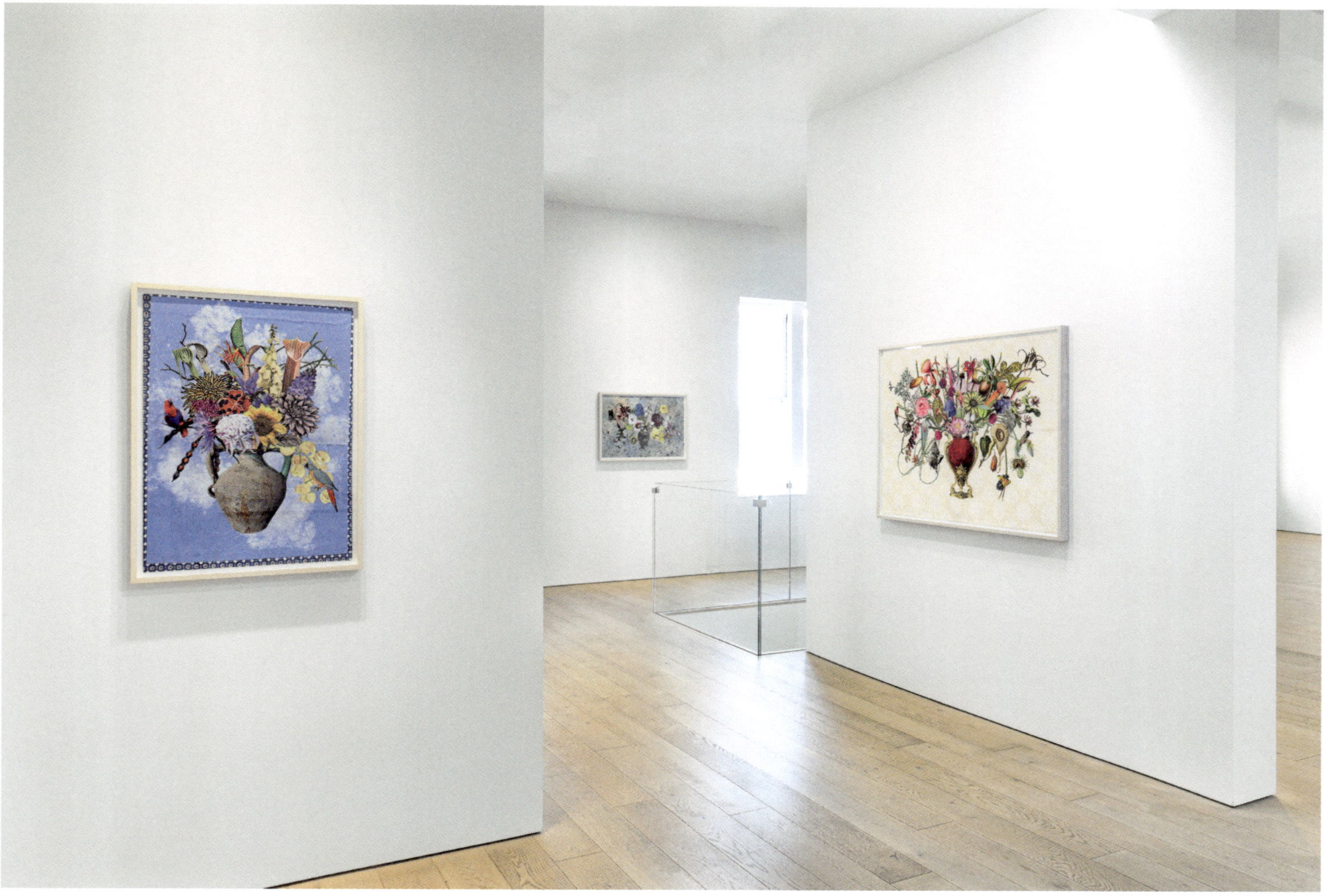

Exhibition views of *Jane Hammond: Chocolate Cosmos, String of Pearls*
Berggruen Gallery, San Francisco
23 October 2025 – 8 January 2026

Contributors

John Berggruen

John Berggruen is an American art collector and dealer who owns Berggruen Gallery in San Francisco. At twenty-six, after working in Democratic campaign politics, Berggruen embarked on what would become a five-decade career as a gallery owner and art dealer. Quickly becoming a nationally recognised gallery in San Francisco, Berggruen Gallery played a major role in shaping the West Coast art scene, acting as an essential bridge between New York, international artists and West Coast collectors and art enthusiasts. Berggruen helped foster the careers of world-renowned artists such as Helen Frankenthaler, Joel Shapiro and Mark di Suvero, and championed prominent California artists including Wayne Thiebaud, Richard Diebenkorn, Nathan Oliveira and Elmer Bischoff, to name a few. The gallery staged ambitious exhibitions of historic significance, featuring works by Alexander Calder, Ellsworth Kelly, Georgia O'Keeffe, Willem de Kooning, Jasper Johns, Robert Motherwell, Robert Rauschenberg, Joseph Cornell, Henry Moore and Henri Matisse. Committed to collecting and exhibiting museum-quality works by the most prominent twentieth and twenty-first-century artists, John Berggruen has made an indelible mark on the broader context of modern and contemporary art in San Francisco and beyond.

Jenny Uglow

Jenny Uglow is an award-winning biographer and historian. A former chair of the council of the Royal Society of Literature, her books include the acclaimed *A Little History of English Gardening*, and she has written on several writers, artists and engravers, including William Hogarth, Thomas Bewick, Walter Crane, Edward Lear and the lino-cut artists Sybil Andrews and Cyril Power. She writes regularly for the *New York Review of Books*, and her most recent book, published in 2025, is *A Year with Gilbert White: The First Great Nature Writer.*

Artist Acknowledgements

A huge thank you to John Berggruen: this book is his brainchild. To the team at Berggruen Gallery: Melanie Ross, Lindsay Salamon, Alexis Kinney, Sloane Black, Mary Kate Tankard, Stephanie Parashis, Jen Loman, Travis Collinson, Ari Ohara, Jillian Shea and Jessica Phillips: I thank you all and deeply appreciate the rigour and passion with which you approach my work and your profession. Your zest is contagious. I would also like to thank the late Gretchen Berggruen as she shaped the gallery with which I now collaborate.

I would like to thank Lyndsey Ingram and her eponymous gallery in London. It was she who was the first champion of these botanical collages, and who introduced this work to Jenny Uglow. Jenny is a lion of the literary world and I am beyond honoured that she has written about this work.

I would also like to thank Nancy Sojka, Curator Emeritus of the Detroit Institute of Arts, Dick Solomon of Pace Prints, as well as Master Printer, Ruth Lingen, and my talented assistant, Elle Rotstein. Big thanks to Galerie Lelong New York and Paris – it's been an honour to be part of both programmes all these many years.

To Craig McNeer, my husband, goes very special gratitude for the unceasing cheerleading and devotion to both me and my practice, and for his keen understanding that there is little distinction between the two. He has for decades shared me gracefully with this other lover.

To Jeffrey Scott French whose help with this publication has far exceeded photography alone, and to Francis Atterbury and the entire Hurtwood team: Anneka French, Louise Frith, Joanna Hilton, Roger Jones, Seb Lansdowne and Matt Price; proofreader William Lambie; and designer Alice Daisy Pomfret. Thank you for producing such a beautiful book.

Jane Hammond
Chocolate Cosmos, String of Pearls

Published by Hurtwood Press Limited, London
Part of the *Hurtwood Artist & Gallery Series*

Series editor: Anneka French
Series design: Alice Daisy Pomfret

Project editor: Anneka French
Proofreading: William Lambie
Layout design: Alice Daisy Pomfret
Reprography and production: Hurtwood Press

Each publication in the *Hurtwood Artist & Gallery Series* presents new, recent and selected works by a single artist working nationally and internationally today. Along with a foreword by an established art world professional, the series features specially commissioned essays and interviews with the artist by leading writers, art historians and curators, offering in-depth insight. Central to each publication are the exhibitions and galleries that help to spotlight some of the most engaging artists of today.

Published in 2026 by Hurtwood Press Limited, London

ISBN: 978-1-917627-07-8

Printed and bound in the UK by Gomer using FSC Mix

FSC www.fsc.org MIX Paper | Supporting responsible forestry FSC® C114687

A catalogue record for this book is available from the British Library.

Jenny Uglow's essay was first commissioned by Lyndsey Ingram Gallery in 2018. It has been reproduced, with revisions by Uglow, by kind permission of the gallery.

Cover image: *Francois Rousseau Vase with Swaddled Babies, Flaming Sword and Bells of Ireland*, 2022 (detail)

Published in association with Berggruen Gallery, San Francisco.